MASTER OF ROCK

A Lighthearted Walk Through the Life and Rock Climbing of John Gill

by Pat Ament

Cover photo: John Gill on a hidden overhang in the forest of Dixon Springs, Southern Illinois, 1965. Photo by Lora Sara Frisch.

Back cover photo: John Gill solo climbs at Blacktail Butte (Tetons in background)

Published by **Adventure's Meaning Press**
5620 South 49th Street
Lincoln, Nebraska 68516
phone: (800)-755-0024

ISBN # 1-881663-04-3

Preface

When I wrote *Master Of Rock* in 1976, I was fortunate to have it published by a real professional--Bob Godfrey. My only criticism was that he added the subtitle "the Biography of John Gill." I had rather intended a short, personal perspective of the rock climbing of Gill. The book became almost instantly out of print and a prize for collectors, often selling at used bookstores for a hundred dollars. Many people asked why I didn't reprint the book. My answer was that I was not satisfied with the writing. I was a relative beginner at writing at the time and also, according to a few critics, had injected more of myself into the story than was needed. I hoped to someday rewrite the book completely and make it a true biography. Friends insisted that if I did rewrite the book that I not leave out the best parts of the first book. Many appreciated the descriptions of my particular involvement with Gill.

And so in this sacred task of trying to make a study of John Gill's life, and attempting to share the remarkable vision that he defines, I have tried to please a number of audiences: those that liked the first book in every way, the boulderers who study the photos and use them as a kind of guide to different climbing areas, and, simply, individuals who are readers of life and literature. In addition, I have tried to make as the soul of the book the lighthearted spirit of Gill, his hilarious stories and wonderful, small points of humor.

I am grateful to John Gill for sharing with me the events of his life and for his assistance with the writing of the book. I am also grateful to Dorothy Gill for her photos and textual insights. I must express my thanks to others who contributed: Chris Jones, Jim

Holloway, Curt Shannon, Lew Hoffman, Warren Banks, Bob Williams, Pete DeLannoy, Paul Muehl, Scott Blunk, John Sherman, and also all the original contributors to the first edition, Dave Rearick, Paul Mayrose, Steve Wunsch, Paul Piana, Bob Candelaria, Bob Kamps, Tom Higgins, David Breashears, Yvon Chouinard, Jim Erickson, and Bob Godfrey.

We have left the majority of the photos in this book uncredited, since most were offhand snapshots by people or friends from the past whose names would require, at best, a guess. However, a large number of the book's older photos, taken during the 1960's, were by Lora Sara Frisch. And Rich Borgman certainly must have taken a few of the photos from Fort Collins.

I am also very grateful to Ed Serr for his help with the layout and word processing of this book.

-- Pat Ament
May, 1992

I dedicate this book to

Shannon Wade

who lifts our spirits

John Gill, Fort Collins, Colorado, early '70s

John Gill became known in the early 1960's for the sheer side of a thirty-foot spire, the Thimble, in the Black Hills of South Dakota, and then for years continued to capture the awe of climbers throughout the world by setting a standard of physical prowess that included the ability to do a one-arm pullup from only one finger. Stories characterized Gill as one who seemed to defy the pull of gravity and, almost more important, who defied the pull of vanity--a man with a stately voice and dignity, yet who never presumed that his activities deserved notice in the mainstream of climbing.

In fact, Gill was somewhat shunned in the late 1950's and early '60s because the scope of his climbing consisted largely of smaller boulders or obscure solo climbs in the Tetons. Gill was beyond the grasp of the somewhat limited mentality of many climbers during that era.

At the peak of his form, and many years before the climbing world could comprehend such a level of ability, Gill pursued his goals in relative solitude, mastering these short rock faces, "boulder problems," and training himself to the far edge of his human, physical capabilities.

Along with his rational and earnest cultivation of gymnastic strengths, Gill clearly possessed a natural physical gift. Another climber trying to follow every step of Gill's training might fall far short of Gill's performance on rock. As with great artistry, it was impossible for Gill to be the subject of imitation. Even super-star climbers today have found themselves groping with an idea that somehow they approach Gill's mastery. Those assumptions are shattered by attempting some of Gill's more difficult routes and by remembering that he did it by himself, without the influence of a community of competitors, when there was no peer inspiration, to speak of, and at a time when the consciousness of climbing was embryonic compared to how extensive it now is.

Yet bouldering always was, for Gill, rooted in the joyful, simple creativity of play. His achievements have been battles in wit that deepen, upon reflection, to subtle espousals of philosophy. Critical to that philosophy has been a strong appreciation of nature: sky, streams, wildlife, differing colors of the rock, hills delicately in bloom, and the forests and air.

As a junior in high school, in 1953, Gill was enticed into climbing by a friend, Jeannie Shearer (later the secretary of the American Alpine Club for several years), who spoke of Indian treasure lost for centuries in the wooded and rolling mountains of northern Georgia. According to an intriguing legend (described by an archaeologist in an article in the Atlanta Constitution), a cave could be found in Fort Mountain at the southern end of the Appalachians. The cave's entrance, hidden midway up a set of forested limestone cliffs (the Beehive cliffs), was marked by a carved turkey-claw. A small group of friends packed sandwiches and a nylon rope and set off toward the fabled cliffs. For footwear, Gill wore floppy, high-top basketball shoes.

The treasure they discovered was "the primordial appeal of climbing on steep rock, stimulated by exposure"--as Gill would later write. The scent of mountain laurels was in the air. Lichen skittered down the gray limestone face as they moved from hold to hold. It was an activity so astoundingly different from traditional southern pastimes that it was next to impossible to discuss their experiences with parents and peers.

Gill's mother, Bernice Alman Gill, was a "typical southern belle" from an authentic southern family that went back several generations and could be traced to the pilgrims. His father, John Paul Gill, was a mathematics instructor at the University of Alabama, one of seven children who grew up in a small coal-mining community, Warrior Run, in Pennsylvania.

Gill's father worked his way through high school. Getting through high school in those days (he was born in 1910) was an accomplishment--comparable to getting through college today. He worked in a mine during the week, taking care of horses that pulled the carts. Deep in the mine was a small stable in which the horses lived, and he fed and watered them while studying his high school lessons throughout the night by lantern. His working these awkward hours did not destroy his scholastic efforts, as he became valedictorian at his high school. He gave his money to his mother to save for him, and she set it aside so that he would have money for college. John senior was the only member of his family who went to college: a year at Penn State and then to the warmer climate of the University of Alabama. He completed his degree while supporting himself as a campus cop. Pursuing his master's degree, he met his wife-to-be, Bernice Alman, who also was a student (a "cotton top," as she described herself) at the University of Alabama. She took a mathematics class from him. Not long after, they were married.

John Gill Jr. was born in February of 1937 in Tuscaloosa, Alabama.

As a fourth-grader in Tuscaloosa, Gill lived with his parents in the country in a little garage apartment in the middle of a large field. He walked to school along a forest path, and through these woods, going and coming, especially coming back in the afternoon, Gill began to develop a feeling for solitude in the outdoors. Several friendly dogs that lived near his house came and met him every afternoon in the forest as he returned home, his first outdoor companions.

The family moved to Houston, Texas, and lived for two years in a suburb called Galena Park. A creek flowed through a wooded lot and through a culvert under the road about two houses from John's. He would look into the culvert, sometimes shine a light down it, and on occasion could see a couple of large, red eyes staring back at him. He and friends thought this was a large bullfrog and threw things into the culvert or let things drift down, in hopes of a response. Later that spring, a heavy rain flooded the culvert and washed up an eight-foot alligator. All in all, John preferred the friendly Tuscaloosa dogs as outdoor companions.

During the summer, walking down a dirt road that bordered another wooded park about half a mile or so from where Gill lived, he encountered large ponderosa pines, a lot of warm sunshine, light striking the forest floor, pine needles lying around, and, within a one block distance, approximately twenty sizable timber rattlesnakes curled up and basking in the heat.

John senior decided to get a Ph.D. in economic statistics and enrolled at the University of Texas in Austin. The young Gill went to an Austin elementary school and then to a junior high school. After class, in a playing field near the junior high, by a stream, he and a few others met on a regular basis with a couple of black students who weren't allowed to attend this school at the time. Gill enjoyed playing football and baseball with these friends.

At age twelve, with no serious objective in mind, John started scrambling on the walls and pillars around the campus of the University of Texas. It seemed adventurous and exciting, until campus security chased him off. He and his parents then moved to Florida where his father took a job as a young assistant professor at Florida State University in Tallahassee. They lived in the country, surrounded by wooded farm land, where John and his friends would taunt bulls--then run to a barn and climb to the loft.

As a boy, Gill spent many summers with his grandparents at their home in Gulfport, Mississippi. He reminisces about these times:

> *"My room above the front porch had a series of windows along the front side, facing south--toward the ocean several blocks away. I would lie in bed reading Ellery Queen, Thorne Smith, Kipling, and others until one or two in the morning, a soft, cool breeze coming through the open windows. Sometimes late at night, thunderstorms rolled in off the Gulf with wild, shrieking winds, rain or hail, and crashing thunder.*
>
> *"I loved to fish in the Gulf. I would rise at 5 a.m. and walk to the large shipping harbor, buy a half pound of fishing-shrimp, and spend the early morning casting my line into the ocean. I fished in the afternoons when it appeared that a storm was moving in. Casting into the rising breakers, I could catch peculiar fish driven in toward land by the approaching weather--weird creatures I was reluctant to cook or eat.*
>
> *"When I was twelve, I was possessed by the idea of catching a shark. The harbor was deep and the water a dark, almost opaque green. I didn't know what quiet giants cruised its depths, but I had once seen a large alligator gar--perhaps two hundred pounds--that was taken there. Tales existed of huge hammerheads. I bought a thin nylon rope and a giant metal hook (several inches long) with an evil barb on its tip. Cane grew in my grandparents' yard, and I cut a six-foot long, two-inch diameter, piece for my pole. I then cut a section of a two-by-four for a float and took a large nut from Grandad's workshop for a weight. In the early morning, I bicycled out to the harbor, and as far*

out as I could along one side of it, to a series of large pilings spaced every four feet or so and rising eight feet out of the water. At one time, these had supported a pier. Now there were only a few planks left, and I was forced to jump from one to the other to get to the outermost. I baited my hook with a freshly caught fish, tossed my heavy line in, and sat down on one of the posts, ready for whatever might come. The waters were still, and I was far out on a peninsula--well away from others.

"After a wait of twenty minutes or so, my wooden block slipped below the surface. I pulled at the pole. It was like trying to stop a submarine. The float reappeared, movement stopped, and I realized I was in over my head. I quickly detached the rope from the pole and tied it around the solid piling I straddled. There, that was more secure. Let's see what happens. Very slowly, the float sank beneath the surface again. The line played out this time at a steady pace and became taut, pulling against my perch. My sense of security was brief, however, for the piling began moving. I scrambled to my feet and jumped to the next piling, barely keeping my balance. When my former post reached a forty-five degree angle, the rope broke. My tackle drifted off into the harbor, vanishing beneath the surface, then reappearing some distance away, until it was finally gone.

"At a different area, at a landing for swimmers reached by a lengthy pier, I swam with porpoises in shallow, translucent waters. You couldn't see the porpoises, but what a thrill when they brushed up against you.

"Grandad had a tiny grocery store and gas pump about a block from the beach. I worked part-time as a clerk and eagerly awaited Thursdays when the new comics would come in. I would carefully read of the latest adventures of the Spirit, and of the Blackhawks, and that great American hero the Fighting Yank.

"There was a small resort and medical clinic across a vacant lot from my grandfather's store, and the owners had a large, fierce-looking Doberman named Midnight. Midnight had a black Scotty companion, and for some *strange reason these two would get out every night about eleven or so. Sometimes I would sneak out and meet these two wonderful creatures, and we would race through the night--down quiet, residential streets that were softly illuminated by a full moon and lampposts, breezes off the Gulf stirring bamboo leaves and the high crests of oaks.*

"In 1951, when I was fourteen, I would sneak down the stairs of my grandparents' house at midnight, out the back door, and across to the garage where grandad kept his new black Dodge with Fluid Drive. I would stealthily open the large doors and push the heavy car out into the alley, then wait for a steam engine locomotive that was always faithfully on schedule. The engine would pass by two blocks away, and sleepers accustomed to the rhythms of the tracks would never hear a car being started. I would drive up and down the coastal highway for fifteen or twenty minutes, then quietly drive the car back into the garage and close and lock the doors. (When I was a father many years later, I would sometimes check the odometer of my own car in the evening and on the following morning.)

"Other images from Gulfport, Mississippi.... I recall listening attentively to a seaman who was staying at my grandparents' house. He told me stories of his wartime adventures and gave me a genuine steel knife from his ship's mess, a utensil I later honed to a razor's edge and hid away.

"Slipping one day into a boarded-up, decaying antebellum mansion, expecting to find only dust and cobwebs, I instead was startled by post-Civil War decor untouched for many years--velvet drapes and chandelier, faded Persian rugs, and a trunkful of clothing--including a confederate uniform and sword. The mansion was blown into splinters by hurricane Camille twenty years later. "

In 1952, Gill's father accepted a teaching position at the University of Georgia in downtown Atlanta. Soon after, in 1953, John met Jeannie Shearer and had his initial experience with rock climbing: in search of lost treasure among the limestone cliffs of northern Georgia.

He visited north Georgia on several more occasions, including a few trips with his father who belayed the rope as John climbed. John's father was supportive but uneasy about this radical new activity his previously unathletic son seemed so fond of.

North Georgia, 1953

North Georgia, 1954

North Georgia

After graduating from high school, Gill and Dick Wimer, one of John's friends from the little Georgia climbing group, planned a trip west to the bigger mountains of Colorado. Dick had climbed in Rocky Mountain National Park and wanted to return. John's father later admitted to John--to the amusement of them both--that he took out a burial policy on his adventurous offspring!

So in 1954, Dick Wimer and Gill drove out from Atlanta in a convertible "Model A" to climb and hike in the mountains of Colorado. The car had non-hydraulic brakes, and Gill found it electrifying when he first took the wheel on a precipitous mountain highway.

They were joined by another friend in Boulder and teamed for an ascent of the Maiden. Here Gill, at age seventeen, had his first taste of legitimate rock climbing. He became the middle man of a three-man ascent of the standard route up the Maiden and was fascinated if not somewhat intimidated by the exposure of the magnificent free-rappel from the spire's summit. They also did the thirteen hundred-foot Third Flatiron above Boulder, then drove to Estes Park and to Meeker Park where they camped.

Gill had been told of the popular Longs Peak, rising into the cold, high-altitude air a few miles north of their camp. He wanted to climb the mountain via the formidable, two-thousand foot, granite East Face. Dick had broken his leg on Longs the previous year, wasn't ready to go back, and did not feel good about Gill trying it. But John wanted a real mountain experience and informed his partner that he was going to do the climb the next day.

5 The East Face of Longs Peak

The seventeen-year-old Gill got up in the morning at 4 o'clock and hitchhiked to the road leading to the Longs Peak campground. The weather looked suitable. He walked the six steep miles to the base of the East Face, having in the way of gear a fifty-foot length of manilla rope, an ice-axe, and his first climbing shoes--J.C. Higgins workboots. He'd had the type of lug rubber soles that mountain climbers used in those days put on the boots.

The route he chose started up the left side of the face, on the Mill's Glacier buttress. His skills were unpolished, but the thrill of exploration was overwhelming--setting his whole body vibrating with energy. In a steep couloir, he suddenly arrived at what appeared to be an impasse. Seeing a knob of rock above, he doubled his rope and threw it up. It caught on the knob, and he pulled himself hand over hand past this obstacle! In a state of intense excitement, he arrived at Broadway--the large ledge halfway up the wall. He was awed by the sweeping verticality of the Diamond--the upper, right-hand portion of the east wall. At that time, climbers questioned whether the thousand-foot Diamond ever would be scaled. The Window route, to the left of the Diamond, had only just been done.

It appeared suddenly that another climber was coming up to Broadway from below, so Gill waited. The other person arrived, dressed in an alpine outfit with knickers, a little cap, and heavy sweater. He introduced himself to Gill as Al Hazel, a local guide. Al said that he was scheduled to replace the summit register and had planned to go up the easy cables route, or via the keyhole, but had spoken with Bob Frossen--the Longs Peak head ranger. Informed by Wimer that Gill was up there by himself, Frossen was furious. People weren't supposed to do that sort of thing. So the guide had agreed to take a look. From a high point on the trail, he was able to spot Gill.

The two talked for a few minutes, and the guide saw that Gill wasn't simply a wild teenager seeking thrills, that Gill had some idea of what he was doing and where he was going. They continued up as a team and, using Gill's fifty-foot rope, tied together for part of the upper portion of the climb. The summit register was replaced, and they started down the cables route. Hazel had a painful trick knee that went out, and Gill's ice-axe served, fortunately, as a cane for the many slow miles back to civilization.

As they approached the ranger station, the guide said, "You wait here, I better clear the way for you." He went down and talked to the ranger. After about fifteen minutes, he returned and said, "O.K., you can come down." He gave Gill a ride back to the campground where Dick Wimer was angry that John had gone ahead and done such a serious climb alone. Wimer referred to him sarcastically as "twinkletoes," an appellation Gill shrugged off.

Tensions subsided after two or three days, and they decided in fact to climb the peak together via the cables route.

Gill at the summit of Longs Peak, after his ascent of the cable route

Following this ascent, they did a number of other classic peaks in the park and also went to the Maroon Bells--an isolated and lovely area at the time. There were only two other people at Mirror Lake when Gill and Wimer ascended the Bells via a traditional route.

During the fall of 1954, Gill enrolled at Georgia Tech and became "a rambling wreck from Georgia Tech" who drank his whisky clear, as the song goes. He was "irrevocably hooked on rock climbing" and investigated the campus for climbing possibilities.

He borrowed his father's car and with a friend drove several times up to Cloudland Canyon, in remote north Georgia, to explore and climb on the canyon walls. Although a state park, there were few people if any around during the fall and spring. On their first trip here, Gill rappelled down into the canyon, some distance away from the camping area, over a hundred-foot cliff and into brush and dense woods. As he stood next to the wall, he heard movement and caught a glimpse of a jacket and glint of steel. He didn't need to think it over. He hurried along the base of the cliff until he found a break in the wall where he could scramble rapidly up a chimney and back to the top. He and his friend looked over the edge but could see no one.

The next morning at daybreak, and approaching the cliffs, they saw several wisps of smoke rising from the dense forest below. They judiciously found another set of cliffs to climb in a side canyon. John later talked with an old, retired state ranger who said that the smoke was from illegal moonshine stills. If in the vicinity of the smoke one dropped a bucket on a rope over the edge of the cliff, with five dollars in the bucket, a tug would be felt after a few minutes. Lifting the bucket out would bring the moonshine purchase. The old ranger added, "If you go into the woods near the stills, you will be shot and killed." Shades of "Deliverance."

Gill leading at Cloudland Canyon, 1954

As a freshman at Tech, Gill was required to take three physical education courses. The most formidable of these was swimming, where Fred Lanoue--who had taught naval aviators to survive under critical conditions--required students to become "drown-proof." A swimmer's hands and feet were bound (hands behind the back). The student had then to jump into the deep end of the pool and swim back and forth across the pool without touching the walls or the bottom. After undergoing this ordeal, Gill showed only "modest talent" in the second course: track. He ran a tremendous 440, pulling away from the pack early, but fell exhausted twenty feet from the finish line. Even after a summer of hiking and climbing, he had not learned to pace himself and exhibited an impulsiveness that would later occasionally put him in precarious positions in rock climbing.

But gymnastics, the third course, appealed to him because of its possible application to climbing. He had a flair for certain pulling exercises, the most notable being the twenty-foot rope climb-- starting in a sitting position with the legs extended and using only arms to ascend.

Once or twice a week, after studying until about 10:30 or 11:00 in the evening, he and a friend crawled stealthily up various buildings and other structures of the Georgia Tech campus. Gill was beginning to use gymnastic chalk for climbing and used it on these buildings. A particular night in 1955, they climbed to the top of a slender, overhanging light tower on the football stadium. They then lowered their army surplus, nylon rappel rope to the distant parking lot below, and John began to rappel. Halfway down the rappel, the approaching headlights of a campus patrol car illuminated the roadway not far away. Quickly pulling up the rope and holding it in his lap, Gill hung silently in the shadows, turning gently in a soft breeze, as the vehicle crept past directly below.

The evening prior to a nationally broadcasted football game, the two darkly-clothed climbers strung a line between two light towers and in the middle of the line hung a gigantic piece of paper with a huge eye painted on it. A fad had been going through the undergraduate culture, having to do with a mysterious, threatening, phantom eye.

They climbed on the administration building, a Victorian structure with nooks and crannies, little towers, and odd projections. It was somewhat scary, because portions of the building were treacherously unstable. They had an excellent time on these outings, often coming back at about 12:30 or 1:00 in the morning.

The second year at Georgia Tech, in 1955 and '56, Gill had become a member of a fraternity and, while living in the fraternity house, introduced a couple of other people to climbing. They went out on Saturdays to Stone Mountain, a seven hundred-foot granite monolith in the woodlands near Atlanta. Neither he nor his two best fraternity friends had a car at the time, so they rented bicycles and rode to Stone Mountain. Considerable effort was required to get there and back, because of the hilly terrain, but adventure and fun far outweighed the exertions of the journey. At the finish of a day's climbing, they bicycled to a restaurant along the highway, had a steak dinner, huge glasses of ice tea, and arrived back at the fraternity house at about two hours before midnight.

Cables and scaffolding from a partially completed Confederate memorial on the vertical north face of Stone Mountain swayed gently overhead as he and friends worked on short, technical face climbs at the bottom of the wall. While climbing, they could hear these rusty girders creak, swaying back and forth, in the wind. It was the only sound except for the wind in the trees. Gill remembers being astounded to find a Holubar piton lying on a ledge below the large, silent, granite soldiers. "It was hard to imagine other climbers in Georgia in the mid '50s."

On one of his early visits to Stone Mountain, still wearing basketball shoes, he bandoliered a rope around his chest and started to lead up gradually steepening rock. There was considerable lichen, and the rock was smooth. He climbed to the steepest point, lost frictional contact, and slid forty feet back to the bottom, skinning his chin and fingers and putting a rough finish on his new nylon rope.

John and his dad hiked around Stone Mountain together on several occasions. The area then was peacefully devoid of people. In the clear, cool Georgia fall, under a deep blue sky, they scared the foxes out of holes, studied eagles and hawks, and picked wild grapes that grew among the rocky outcrops.

During his stay at Georgia Tech, John took a long trip west with his parents and drove through the Black Hills of South Dakota. Gill's first acquaintance with the Needles, he got out of the car and soloed a couple of easy spires. It seemed exciting to him. They also visited the majestic Teton range of Wyoming. Gill wanted to climb one of the Tetons and met several members of the Princeton Mountaineering Club who were planning to go up the east face of Teewinot the next day. He joined with them, climbed Teewinot, and then he and his parents drove to Colorado where he scrambled around on some crags near McGreggor rock in Rocky Mountain National Park.

As a member of the Georgia Tech gymnastics team for a brief time, Gill performed the speed rope-climbing event. Don Perry, a rope-climbing inspiration during the 1950's, had set a speed record of 2.8 seconds for twenty feet--faster than most people could pull a loose rope on the floor between their legs. Gill's fastest unofficial time, attained after he had left Tech, was 3.4 seconds. Besides Perry, Gill was taken with the great Russian gymnast Albert Azaryin. At Leow's Grand Theater in downtown Atlanta--site of the premier of "Gone With The Wind"--Gill saw a newsreel of a still-ring routine performed by Azaryin and envisioned translating such strength to rock climbing. He immediately became especially fond of the rings and worked both flying and still-rings for a number of years. Not afraid to take a calculated risk, Gill performed the dangerous cut-and-catch on the front swing of the flying rings. He also executed the flying cross.

He transferred to the University of Georgia after two years, preferring its mathematics program, and joined the Air Force R.O.T.C. No gymnastics team existed at the University of Georgia, but apparatus were available to John and several gymnastic friends.

In '56, he got a summer job for two months with the forest service in Bend, Oregon, establishing "P"-lines for road surveys, laying out boundary lines for timber sales, clearing brush, burning slash, and pruning trees. He climbed several mountains while in Oregon, including Mount Thielson by the South Face, wearing basketball shoes. He then took a bus to the Tetons and climbed for about three weeks.

Gill saw serious Teton rock climbers for the first time on the Jenny Lake boulders, people such as Dick Emerson, Richard Pownall, and Willi Unsoeld. Emerson was a ranger at the time, Pownall and Unsoeld guides. Gill noticed them putting forest duff--the powdery residue on the base of the forest--on their hands to dry their hands before they started up the rock. He realized at this point that gymnastic chalk was indeed the ideal thing for this. He started using it consistently, introducing it to east and west coast climbers who were in the Tetons.

Occasionally pulling from his pocket a piece of chalk to rub on his hands, he climbed the north face of Teewinot with a friend, the north face of Cloudveil Dome, a number of other longer Teton climbs, and a few isolated rock climbs of modest severity.

Gill on Hangover Pinnacle, in the Tetons, 1957

One summer after climbing for several weeks, John hitched a ride into Jackson with his steamer trunk full of clothing and climbing equipment. He rented a tent frame only a block or two from the town square and was given an old bell-type alarm clock and several thick, patchwork quilts, since the evenings were quite cold. Jackson still had at that time a somewhat "authentic" appearance, as opposed to its current cosmopolitan ambience (with jet liners circling). The Hollywood movie "Shane" had recently been filmed in Jackson Hole. In the '50s, a stage ran from Jackson Hole to Rock Springs. This was an old bus from the '40s, driven by a cowboy who looked like Gary Cooper. In the morning, Gill caught the stage. Halfway to Rock Springs, a cowboy passenger got drunk and became belligerent. The driver stopped the bus, pulled the character off, dumped him on the ground, got back in, and drove off--all without saying a word. John Wayne, where are you today?

Athens, Georgia, 1957

John graduated from the University of Georgia in 1958, with a degree in mathematics, and received a commission in the Air Force. He was scheduled to report to the University of Chicago in October of the following fall for a twelve-month sequence of courses in meteorology. This would prepare him to serve as a weather officer. But he had a free summer before this educational commitment was to begin and so worked for a month, then spent a month climbing in the Tetons where he explored the buttresses of Garnet Canyon and succeeded at twelve or thirteen probable first ascents. These were formations anywhere from 200 feet to 800 or 900 feet in length, ranging in difficulty from 5.2 to 5.10--a degree of severity that had not yet been invented anywhere else in America at the time! It might be pointed out that some of the hardest of these pitches were "optional" (contrived at points where other choices were available).

Gill camped and bouldered with Yvon Chouinard in 1958 and swears he saw a bird commit suicide in Yvon's three-day old dishwater. The bird took a drink and then collapsed.

Chouinard talks about Gill:

> I don't remember when I met Gill. Must have been the late '50s. There were few climbers in the Tetons in those days, mainly people from the eastern colleges, Dartmouth, Harvard.... Climbers on their way to expeditions in Alaska or somewhere would stop through the Tetons. A handful of people were climbing intensively in the Tetons and lived there the whole summer, scrounging on fifty cents a day, eating oatmeal.... At that time, Gill was doing some climbs on Disappointment Peak. After grabbing whatever climbing partner he could find, he'd do some little arete that often wouldn't lead anywhere, because Disappointment Peak is just a big flat thing on top. Kamps and I did Satisfaction Buttress, and it was the hardest climb in the Tetons when we did it, yet the *American Alpine Journal* refused to publish anything about it because it didn't have a summit. That was where climbing was, in those days. If it didn't have a summit, you really didn't do a climb. Gill was getting even more ridiculous and was doing things just for the sake of pure climbing, going nowhere. These were absurd climbs, as far as the Alpine Club was concerned. Now people do a one-pitch climb, and it's a route, so I guess he was ahead of his time in that respect.
>
> When a party would go to repeat a route Gill had given a 5.8 or 5.9 rating they would find it to be 5.5, because Gill had done some unlikely variation which they could not discover. He wouldn't do the most logical way. He'd go out and enjoy himself on hard problems.
>
> I did a couple routes with him on...the Knob? These were several-pitch, roped climbs. At that time, he was a smooth climber, always under control. But he didn't seem to be a bold climber. There are some people who are extremely bold who aren't exceptional physical climbers, but boldness gets them up the climb. Maybe Gill didn't need to be bold then. He used to do a lot of roped leads,

although I don't think he ever really cared for it. He enjoyed bouldering much more and, I believe, was happier when he realized that. It may have tended to make him a bit insecure that everyone else was climbing with a rope. He chose to specialize in one form of climbing, pure bouldering and, specifically, overhanging face climbing. He loved overhangs. He never really got into crack climbing.

Gill and I developed some of the climbs on the boulders in the Tetons. We named the boulders and worked on them for hours at a time. Falling Ant Slab was named because the angle was such that ants would go up, reach a point, and peel off! There was a route called "Cut-Finger" where you had to use a hold that would...cut your finger. There were sharp quartz crystals, and you'd come back from a day of bouldering with your hands in shreds. That's why we called one boulder Red Cross Rock. I could do pretty many of the climbs in those days, but three or four I didn't have a chance with. He had well over a foot reach on me. The only thing I used to get him on were occasional no-hands routes. I had a much lower center of gravity. But when I first bouldered with Gill, he was nowhere as good as a few years later. He was getting better very fast.

We wrote a little guidebook to the Jenny Lake boulders. Gill did the drawings for it and the gradings of the routes. I wrote the text. It's a classic. The rangers have the one copy and guard it. We wrote it tongue in cheek and patterned it after the guide to the Tetons which says, "These mountains are big mountains, they make their own weather." We wrote the same about the boulders: "These are big boulders, they make their own weather." We talked about the north faces and the big south faces.

We'd take visiting climbers to the boulders on rainy days and show them the routes. Gill and I shared the same campsites and would go together to Blacktail Butte. Blacktail Butte is gray limestone, absolutely 90 degrees, all finger holds. I remember the third route he did there. I'm sure it's 5.10. It may have been one of the first 5.10 routes in the country, because that was about 1959 or so. It's one of those things where you've got to go quickly and you've got to conserve strength. Your forearms get pumped up. Of course he didn't have to go very fast, because his arms never gave out.

Gill rediscovered Baxter's Pinnacle in the Tetons. It had been climbed with direct-aid by Baxter and a party from Stanford in the mid-'40s but had been considered lost for a number of years. He told Chouinard about his discovery, and Yvon and a friend did the second ascent with a step or two of direct-aid. Gill and a companion then climbed the spire free. John and another companion later returned to Baxter's Pinnacle and did a difficult variation, "up the left face of the direct-aid crack," a vertical face for fifteen feet or so, perhaps the earliest 5.10 in the country.

He did the first ascent of Delicate Arete, also likely 5.10 (via the optional line Gill took). What made this route scary was its relative lack of protection at a critical section. Also making the second ascent of the route, with Ritner Walling, Gill got into trouble doing a very hard optional move thirty or forty feet above an expansion bolt. A strong wind came up and buffeted him around severely. He had to plaster himself against the rock while on tiny holds. Ritner later described Gill as looking like an ant trying to keep from being blown off by the wind. The wind would cease, and Gill would start to make a move, but all of a sudden he would be blasted by another enormous gust. It would become calm again, and he would start to move, but he would be blasted again from a different direction. The worst lasted a matter of minutes but seemed like an eternity. On those tiny footholds, he was using a pair of early climbing shoes that were good for edging but had no real frictional characteristics. These "Zillertals," from Austria, with hard, black, lug rubber soles, were the "state of the art" in rock shoes at the time.

He established a number of bouldering routes in the Tetons that he later repeated many times, on Red Cross Rock, Falling Ant Slab, and Cutfinger Rock--the so-called Jenny Lake boulders. Gill also made several first ascents on Blacktail Butte, some of these done initially as exploratory free-solo routes.

After the summer of 1958, Gill's focus evolved somewhat away from longer climbs. He followed the dictates of temperament, centering his attention more frequently on small boulders of substantial difficulty. In many cases, of course, smaller rocks were all that were available in the areas in which he lived.

During his year at the University of Chicago, he worked out with the University of Chicago gymnastics team and developed the ability to do a one-arm, one-finger pullup! He began to work on this extraordinary feat as the result of a rumor. Helmut Rohrl, a German mathematician who lived in Chicago and climbed with Gill on occasion, informed John (erroneously) that Hermann Buhl--the great European mountaineer--was able to do a one-finger pullup. In those days, people tended to exaggerate the abilities of their heroes. Gill found it to be a provocative idea. He'd already developed a strong one-arm pullup and in no time added this "finesse."

While stationed in Chicago in 1959, Gill drove five or six times to Devil's Lake--a rock climbing area in Wisconsin. He found chalk useful here because of the slick quartzite, especially during the summer months when it was very humid.

An early visit to Devil's Lake, Wisconsin

Chalk marks on difficult-looking rock faces began to be the mark for other climbers that John Gill had paid a visit.

In 1959, he finished his meteorology training at the University of Chicago and, in the month or so before reporting to Glasgow Air Force Base in northeastern Montana, drove to the Tetons with all his possessions in a Studebaker Power Hawk. He spent several weeks climbing there in late summer, often sneaking up to do a long, covert solo, an activity that was strictly illegal in Grand Teton National Park at the time.

In the Tetons in 1959, he did the first ascent of the center of Red Cross Rock. This was an exceptionally difficult, short problem and the first significant "dynamic route" in America--if not anywhere. Normally climbs were done in a "static" fashion, whereby each move was deliberate and often reversible. Gill was willing to commit himself to physical flight upward, committing himself in aerial feats where he threw his body free of the rock and upward off a hold. This route on Red Cross Rock remains to this day a formidable test piece. John repeated it many times during the years that followed the first ascent.

Red Cross Rock, in the Tetons, Center Overhang (above) and North Corner Overhang (photos taken later in 1965)

By the late '50s, Gill had become the author of countless small, preposterously demanding (however obscure) routes, little incidents of climbing that would later be viewed by the climbing populace as developments far beyond the measure of difficulty anywhere else in the world at the time.

Things would get a little dull as a weather forecaster at Glasgow, and he would walk up into the control tower during evenings shifts and do pullups to pass the time. He kept up his gymnastics at the base gymnasium. He had purchased a speed-climbing rope and a set of rings and hung them in the gym. Every other day, he worked out for one to two hours.

Gill wore a gun sometimes in Glasgow, a .22 magnum Colt Buntline with 9-inch barrel. This was legal at the time. It couldn't be concealed, however. One day in 1960 while walking in downtown Glasgow, Gill's best friend, a Base police officer, saw one of his airmen strolling down the sidewalk sporting two pearl-handled six-guns. Gill's friend discovered that the airman was working as a hired gun for a local rancher and was involved in a ranching feud with the hired guns of another rancher. A couple of men had already been shot. A little of the Old West was still alive in northern Montana in 1960.

During his three years at Glasgow, Gill climbed near Zortman, Montana, in an area called the Little Rockies.

At Zortman, Montana

Zortman was on an Indian reservation. The country was remote and a little wild, the inhabitants unpredictable. Every week or so, one would read of violence. Thus Gill carried his side-arm. He would leave the regular roadway and drive his Studebaker Power Hawk several miles across empty fields to the base of the limestone cliffs. The first time he did this, he stopped beside a gravel road and walked about a hundred yards into a bordering field to check the surface of the ground. An old car pulled diagonally in front of his, and two tough-looking Indians, hard and grim men in their thirties, got out and started walking toward him. One carried a tire iron. Gill was uneasy about this. There was no sign of anyone else for miles, and an Indian had burned down a small school house the previous week. There was a fair amount of hostility between the Anglos and the Indians. Gill stood his ground and stared at them. They stopped when they saw he was armed, stared back for about ten seconds, then turned without a word, walked back to their car, got in, and drove away.

The limestone cliffs that he reached were unstable, and he had trouble finding solid, smooth sections with tiny holds. On one trip, he soloed a hundred feet up an inside corner to the obscure small entrance to a cave. With flashlight, he crouched and crawled inside and found himself in a large, roughly circular, dome-shaped room, perhaps thirty feet in diameter, with a ceiling some twenty feet above a peculiar sandy floor sinking down in its center. As he moved across the soft floor, it started shifting--funneling into a vortex at the center. It was like walking on the top sandy surface of an hourglass. He moved quickly to the wall and climbed onto a small ledge, listening to a distant rumble as sand and debris vanished into the hole. After a few minutes, the floor ceased its movement. He crept gingerly around to the entrance and crawled out. Indiana Jones, eat your heart out.

John would drive down to Fort Peck Dam in good weather, rappel down into the dry causeway, remaining out of sight of the caretaker's cabin, and climb up steep concrete slabs to a point where he could ascend a short overhang and up a vertical wall to the top. The solitude was magnificent, the terrain bleak but attractive. Warm Chinook winds would melt the snow in spring, and in the drying air the brown hills seemed to breathe.

During the winter, and bundled in a wolf-fur parka, he ice skated along the Milk River, barren trees overhanging the frozen stream bed.

John continued to visit the Tetons. Dave Rearick has fond recollections:

> In August, 1960, I spent two or three weeks in the Tetons, at the climbers' campground on the south shore of Jenny Lake which the rangers had created a year or two earlier to try to keep the climbing scene out of the sight of the general public. There's no trace of that campground anymore, except maybe the old kilns that Yvon Chouinard and Ken Weeks were sleeping in; or the big tree in the clearing where one night somebody, likely the Vulgarians, lassoed a bear and pulled him down with a rope attached to a truck; and perhaps the large cement slab of unknown origin is still there, on which for several hours every morning John Gill and I practiced our handbalancing. John was able to do a "stiff-stiff" body press, and I kept working on it: getting a little closer every day with encouragement from John, but never quite succeeding, until finally, right after he left and there was no one to show off for, I did five of them in a row.

For lunch we'd go over to the little general store run by two old ladies and try to absorb as much protein as possible. John favored a thick, pasty mixture of powdered milk as a good muscle-builder, never mind what it tasted like. Afternoons, we had long sessions of hatchet-throwing, along with Bill Woodruff who had bicycled across from Yosemite and was resting up before riding further east.

Later on, John would usually drive over to Blacktail Butte for an hour or two of solo climbing. I never accompanied him there, and few people knew just what he was up to, but Bob Kamps went along once or twice and later told me he couldn't top-rope some of the things John was soloing. As for the little boulders around the campground, there was none, even if only knee-high, that had not felt the tread of John's tightly-laced climbing shoes on whatever tiny crystals or minute features it offered by way of a bouldering problem.

John Gill was a frequent visitor at the Jenny Lake Ranger Station, usually not to sign out for a climb but to practice fingertip front levers on the doorjamb. From the parking lot, all you could see was a pair of long legs extending horizontally out the front door, knees together and toes carefully pointed.

Gill doing a "front lever"

All of his exercises, from the most outrageous bouldering maneuvers down to his frisbee throwing with garbage-can lids, were executed with the utmost control and painstaking attention to style; and all of this, together with his agreeable manner and a certain intriguing reluctance to separate reality from absurdity, made John an outstanding companion for whiling away those long, exuberant summer days.

The Needles of South Dakota

In the spring of 1961, he did the first ascent of the daunting Thimble route. The Thimble, a thirty-foot pinnacle, brought the first real fame to Gill. This sheer, extremely difficult ascent was completed without the use of a rope or any form of protection, completely solo, and risking a fall onto a parking lot guard-railing.

On an earlier visit to the Needles, in 1960, Gill had climbed the Thimble via another route (5.8?) that followed a faint groove on the left side of the actual overhanging wall. He later spotted a possible line of ascent up the steeper face to the right and scrambled halfway up the groove route to look over at the holds on the bulging wall. It became apparent what sorts of moves he would be responsible for if he were willing to commit himself to the climb. He felt that it was time he do something more committing, with more of an element of risk, than the usual difficult but relatively safe boulder routes he enjoyed. The route of which he was thinking was not a suicide mission. There was a possible escape halfway up where he could, if necessary, move left to the easier groove of the original route.

With an image of this unclimbed, overhanging wall of the Thimble in mind, he returned to Glasgow Air Force Base and started to devise ways, around the gym, in which to train for some of the moves that he anticipated doing on the Thimble. He squeezed nuts and bolts sticking out of the gym walls to prepare for the nubbins that he would have to squeeze high up on the Thimble. He could do seven regular one-arm pullups, three finger-tip one-arm pullups, and of course his one-finger/one-arm pullup, and he continued to train at these.

The Thimble remained on his mind during the winter, and he returned to it on leaves from the base. His approach was to climb up and down the bottom half of the route until he had that much wired.

Gill on the Thimble

Once or twice, he jumped from a respectably high point. He had developed skill at leaping down from high places, as related by Richard Goldstone in regard to a different climb:

Gill jumped off from about twenty feet up and landed like a cat in the midst of jagged talus boulders.

At last Gill worked himself "into such a fevered pitch" on the Thimble route that he committed himself to the top portion of it and, as he admitted, "very fortunately made it."

Gill stated later in an interview, "You not only get psyched up but almost become hypnotized or mesmerized to the point where your mind goes blank, and you climb by well-cultivated instincts. You do it." John can't recall if a young airman named Higgins accompanied him on that culminating trip to the Needles. Higgins had certainly served as a spot for Gill at an earlier time on the Thimble.

At the top, knowing it was over, and in a world by himself, Gill felt "a peculiar absence of feeling." Little was said by him about the route, before or after. He did not brag.

the Thimble, with approximate lines drawn in by Gill several
years after the ascent (the difficult route on the right)

At first, when Gill's bouldering in the Tetons and in the Black Hills of South Dakota became known, it was not believed that such routes had intrinsic importance. Size and elevation and glorious summits were more in the spirit of the mainstream focus at the time. Many climbers in the late '50s and early '60s did not want to recognize such extreme artistry when they became aware of it. These routes were, in the estimation of some, merely stunts. In fact Gill's routes were the actions of a private, humble, but nevertheless competitive, individual seeking the simplicity of a disciplined path in a severe, intimidating medium. Also--because of Gill's solitude-- much of what he accomplished remained relatively unknown.

There were tales and rumors around campfires of some kind of mythical person who had mastered an overhanging wall in the Needles or who had done a few difficult solo ascents in Wyoming's Tetons.

Gill relates the following story:
"I was once bouldering in solitude in the Needles, when a young female climber walked up and introduced herself and asked who I was. I told her and continued bouldering. She turned and walked away after a few minutes, saying over her shoulder, 'You can't be John Gill. He climbs much better than that.'"

Gill on "The Incisor," in the Needles, early '60s

Gill on his route on the direct north overhang of the Scab, in the Needles

Of course at other instances there could be no mistaking that one was in the presence of Gill, as in the following account by Paul Mayrose:

This is a tale of a first encounter--stereotyped perhaps, but quite real nevertheless--with John Gill. Bouldering was a new concept around Estes Park, Colorado, in the early 1960's. None of us locals were quite sure how to approach it. It could be entertaining, but should it ever be taken seriously? The answer put in an appearance one pleasant Saturday afternoon.

It was the Hagermeister boulders. I don't remember the cast of characters. Bob Bradley was certainly there, Dave Rearick almost certainly...and perhaps half a dozen others. A person was introduced as John Gill. Mr. Gill was a tall person, quiet, and not particularly impressive physically as long as he stood absolutely still! If he moved in the slightest, he rippled and bulged. I decided that he was healthy.

As the afternoon progressed, so did most of us. Ah, the competitive instinct! Gill got quite far enough off the ground to convince me that bouldering was not any kind of sop for frustrated acrophobiacs. His funny business enabled the rest of us to climb better...without getting overly philosophical.

He climbed, and I watched. He climbed, and we fell off in his wake...in droves. Eventually, I became convinced that he wasn't actually strong enough to cheat by gouging his own holds into the rock. A few of the cast became discouraged and left. I, and others, got mad and determined and stayed...and started getting up occasional things we would not have recognized as climbable that morning.

Bouldering had come to Estes Park in earnest. Basic concepts hadn't been changed, but the order of magnitude certainly had. I took up bouldering. For me it was never an end in itself, but it became the difference between 5.8 and 5.9 (even a little 5.10) on bigger climbs. As always, advance stemmed from one individual who pushed beyond convention. A committee of 5.9 climbers cannot meet and climb 5.10 or anything but 5.9. But one man can. John Gill showed me that levels of climbing could be pushed higher. Knowing him, I went in search of my own limit. Apparently I found it, but I have never since tried to guess the upper bounds for someone else. Not bloody well likely after the shock of a first meeting with Gill.

Gill, Hagermeister Boulders, early '60s

In the course of his one-arm, one-finger pullup training, Gill developed the ability to do it also on the middle finger of his left hand and on the index finger of his right hand! A one-finger pullup set a certain gauge of strength, a most severe task for even the strongest, flyweight gymnasts. Approaching a hundred and ninety pounds and six-foot-two, Gill had no such advantage of lightness. Thus his size made his accomplishments all the more impressive.

Skeptics suggested that Gill was all muscle, a show of strength. But at the Jenny Lake boulders in the Tetons, a number of competent climbers found it difficult to repeat--with the use of all four of their limbs--one of Gill's no-hands routes, where he walked up a steep face of rock, using only feet on small holds.

No-hands route on Falling Ant Slab, in the Tetons

There was no question for anyone who spent time with Gill that his footwork, balance, creativity, problem-solving insight, subtlety, and control were commensurate with his strength. Rich Goldstone, one of Gill's bouldering partners who John had met in Chicago, mentioned that John did a number of "eliminates" in the Shawangunks of New York. A handful of eastern climbers at the time tried everything from karate yells to shoulder stands in determined efforts to succeed. No one did.

Another brief characterization of Gill is offered by Bob Kamps:

> In the Needles in the '60s, I found Gill to be a little aloof or cold. But I can only recall bits and pieces. I remember that Gill drove a little sports car. There was a short, leaning face which Gill was able to climb by starting atop a small, round piece of wood. With this cheater's stick, he was able to reach the first holds of the route. But he wouldn't allow me the use of a ten-foot log to stand on."

Paul Piana speaks also of Gill's presence in the Needles:

> A walk through the Needles would be a relaxing joy suddenly shattered when one of our troupe would spy a tiny, white arrow pointing up an overhanging bulge or smooth slab. The idea that they were drawn in jest faded as we learned more about Gill. We made an ascent of the Thimble's easy side. The summit register said, "Hats off to John Gill," signed by Royal Robbins. Gill had done the overhanging side of the rock, to Royal's and everyone's amazement. A trip to the Spire 1 area gave us our first glimpse of Gill. He was high up, alone on the spire. It was the first solo ascent of the route. Renn Fenton showed us a boulder problem, a smooth, flared, upside-down trough with an arrow, and said that even when Gill strained you didn't know it.

Gill climbs a corner of rock (Amorphous) in the Needles

Paydirt Pinnacle, in the Needles, mid-'60s

When Gill left the Air Force in May of 1962, he packed up all his belongings in a VW sedan he'd purchased in Glasgow and left the base for a summer of climbing and hiking before starting graduate school at the University of Alabama. He drove first to Zion National Park, where he did some climbing and bouldering, then stopped at several places in Colorado, and ended up in the Tetons where he met his wife-to-be, Lora, in the climbing campground. It was early in the season, and she and he were the only people there for several days. He slept in an old-fashioned, Wenzel umbrella tent pitched beneath a tree. Every morning at about five a.m., a squirrel dropped remnants of a pine cone down on the tent, and Gill would drowsily beat the canvas sides. Then the squirrel jumped from a limb three or four feet above the top of the tent onto one side of the tent and slid down it like a slide. It became a regular thing, like nature's alarm clock. Here was another of Gill's outdoor companions.

Lora and John left the Tetons, went to the Black Hills, enjoyed some climbing together, journeyed to Colorado toward the end of this summer of '62, and were married in a magistrate's office in Boulder. They then drove to Alabama to Gill's parents' house in Tuscaloosa where they stayed until they could get a downtown apartment in an old antebellum home. John brewed sake in a tub in the kitchen closet, until the landlady found out, and he watched many hours of Rocky & Bullwinkle between studies.

He returned to graduate school to get a master's degree in mathematics at the University of Alabama, continued gymnastics on his own, and found bouldering in northern Alabama, at locations such as Shades Mountain outside of Birmingham and Desoto Canyon. There were even a few climbing spots around Tuscaloosa, deep in the mossy woods on cement-like conglomerate with huge pebbles.

Shades Mountain, Alabama

Shades Mountain, Alabama

Tuscaloosa, Alabama

Gill found time to visit the Tetons for some bouldering, as related by Jim Erickson:

> In 1963, I am a beginning climber at Devil's Lake, Wisconsin, and experienced climbers tell engrossing stories around the campfires. The name John Gill is attached to tales of a person able to do one-arm pullups while pinching the 2x4's of a basement ceiling. Gill seems to possess more of the qualities of heroic myth than of flesh and blood. Yet climbs at Devil's Lake are there to prove the myths: Gill's Corner, Gill's Crack, Sometime Crack, The Flatiron....
>
> In August of 1964, my brother and I are in the Tetons contemplating the underside of Red Cross Rock--a twelve-or-so-foot, mushroom-shaped boulder. Two figures wander over to us, and we recognize Rich Goldstone whom we know from Devil's Lake. We exchange greetings, and Rich introduces us to his companion, John Gill. Dave and I nearly faint, for we've half-believed that Gill had no corporeal existence. We observe, as the two climbers use mysterious white chemicals on their fingers, mats for their feet, and tiny lichen brushes while devising extreme routes up the boulder.
>
> Finally Gill moves to the north corner overhang, stands on a small foothold, grabs an undercling with his left hand, and reaches with the other hand out over the bulge for what appears to be nothing. He simultaneously springs and does a one-arm, fingertip pullup on this

nothing. Dave and I fail to comprehend what we have seen and, after the two leave, examine that hold. It is about an eighth of an inch wide.

Their second year in Alabama, Lora and John moved to a Tuscaloosa housing development for students. Barracks had been converted into apartments at the site of an old naval base. And although not a particularly attractive place to live, they had the bare necessities. This complex was blown up later in 1977 as part of the filming of the Burt Reynolds movie "Hooper." Gill was delighted to see the very place he had lived go up in smoke.

When Gill finished his master's, they moved to Murray, Kentucky, where their daughter, Pam, was born in 1965. John met several Persians who became friends and who taught him how to play soccer, and there were short rock climbs and bouldering to be found in Southern Illinois at Dixon Springs and in Kentucky at Pennirile Forest State Park. John put up several difficult boulder routes at Dixon Springs, including "Rebuttal"--a smooth, bulging, sandstone wall fifteen feet high. Cave-In Rock State Park, on the Ohio River, was another area John visited. Ray Shragg, Rich Goldstone, and R.F. Williams, climbing friends of Gill's who were living in Chicago, drove down to visit him one Christmas. It was about five degrees at Dixon Springs, with snow on the ground. But they got out, involved themselves in some spirited bouldering, and then drove home via a ferry across the ice-swollen Ohio River.

Gill at Murray, Kentucky

Pennirile Forest, Kentucky

Pennirile Forest

Kentucky

Bell Smith Springs

Cave-In-Rock State Park (on the Ohio River)

Persian Wall, Dixon Springs,

Persian Wall, Dixon Springs, Southern Illinois

A hidden overhang, Dixon Springs

Dixon Springs

In 1967, Gill decided to get a Ph.D. in mathematics. He wanted a school that was near a climbing area, and Colorado seemed an appropriate place. He applied to both the University of Colorado in Boulder and Colorado State University in Fort Collins and liked the offer he received to be a graduate teaching assistant at C.S.U. He would never regret this choice.

While finishing his Ph.D. in the later '60s, Gill climbed a great deal with a student and university gymnast by the name of Rich Borgman. Just before being kicked out of the gymnastic room because he wasn't a team member, Gill was told by the gymnastics coach that there was a climber "who could crawl all over the walls without any visible holds." This piqued Gill's curiosity. The two finally met and climbed together extensively on the solid, yellow-brown, Dakota sandstone running along ridges near Horse Tooth Reservoir west of Fort Collins. No bouldering had been previously done there, and Rich and John put up dozens of routes--a paradise of virgin rock.

Rich Borgman, Fort Collins, Colorado

I was a gymnast fifty miles south at the University of Colorado in Boulder and competed against Rich in a gymnastic meet near the time I was fortunate to become another of Gill's bouldering companions.

I had heard of Gill as far back as the early '60s and on a climbing trip to the Needles of South Dakota saw his route, his turning of the soul, on The Thimble. I could see that the climb was a total and complete commitment. Skeptics who had put Gill down as a "mere boulderer" were of little consequence in the light of one very positive soul who pursued his personal goals, cognizant of, but undisturbed by, the views of others. It must have been something to behold--if anyone was there to watch--Gill's strength and balance approaching their limits, hands tightening, feet edging ingeniously on fragile pebbles.

With Gill at Horse Tooth Reservoir, west of Fort Collins, in 1968, I mis-timed a lunge and fell onto a talus boulder onto my tailbone. Gill expressed genuine concern and was relieved to find that I was not injured seriously. Shaky, I continued in the role of observer for the remainder of the bouldering session and watched Gill and Rich climb overhang after overhang.

Gill in Boulder, Colorado, photo by Pat Ament

In 1968 at Split Rocks, a wonderful garden of boulders located on a forest hillside approximately twenty miles northwest of Boulder, Gill and I climbed the better part of a day. Jagged granite blocks strewn throughout the pines wore the flesh of our fingertips and shredded our egos. A warm sun made the day pleasant, and we invented many sorts of problems. I realized that there was more training in store for me, that I would have to return to the area, to be able to do a couple of the routes that Gill ascended with authority.

Low and commanding, his voice was rarely heard except for an occasional deep chuckle in response to my exertions. He approached a smooth, overhanging, fifteen-foot wall and, at first, gently drew breath. Then his eyes became fixed upon a high hold. While compressing his upper torso, as if to recoil, he began to breathe rapidly. To follow was a perfectly calculated, slow-motion leap. There was a subtle, although important, shuffling of his feet on tiny nubbins. One hand reached over the rounded summit, the other pulled laterally. It was quick, and he was at the top of the boulder.

I squeezed the initial holds and sighed. I could grasp the holds but not the problem. Gill tried to dispel my romantic notions, insisting that he had lots of weaknesses and that I was the real climber because I did longer routes and big-wall ascents. We rigged a top-rope, and Gill belayed me on a "delicate wall." I got a hand on the hold at the top before my weight went onto the rope. On a later visit to Split Rocks, I made the delicate wall and repeated it again on subsequent visits because the route seemed to bring Gill to me when he was not there.

Gill on the Delicate Wall

"So strong and directed is Gill's presence," my friend Tom Higgins noted. Almost in a ghostly way, thoughts of Gill followed me everywhere. Even as I watched an issue of the T.V. series "Star Trek," Captain Kirk had a confrontation with John Gill--"the Fuhrer."

Gill's mastery went beyond merely overcoming difficulty and was defined also by the relaxed, controlled manner in which he ascended intimidating routes.

Tucked innocuously into the pages of the 1969 *American Alpine Journal* was Gill's first climbing article, called "The Art Of Bouldering," wherein he explained that bouldering was not merely practice for longer routes. It was an art in its own right, in the spirit of gymnastic competition: "...the boulderer is concerned with form almost as much as with success and will not feel that he has truly mastered a problem until he can do it gracefully."

In that article, Gill listed a few skills that might be developed by a serious boulderer, including one-arm mantel presses, one-arm pullups with a hand squeezing a beam, one-arm finger-tip chins on doorjambs, and one-arm/one-finger pullups on a bar. As a gymnast, he had learned moves such as the "inverted iron cross" and, also on the still-rings, the slow, straight-body pull from a hang to a handstand. His favorite ring maneuver was the "butterfly mount," through an L-cross, an exercise beginning with a straight-arm hang and pulling into an iron cross. He pointed out that these skills were not absolutely necessary for bouldering but might add a certain polish to one's climbing!

Gill climbs the left side of the Eliminator, Fort Collins

The left side of the Eliminator

Climbing was, for Gill, an extension of gymnastics. In his backyard in Fort Collins, Colorado, he set up a few pieces of apparatus for working out. He was able to do a one-arm pullup while holding his 30-pound daughter and taught himself--perhaps invented--the one arm front-lever, a position where the body is held horizontally in the air while hanging from one straight arm. Gill applied this particular skill to routes at Horse Tooth Reservoir that required a kind of extended leverage, with arms out on either side of the body, pressing up on fingertip holds.

One-finger pullup and one-arm front
lever, Fort Collins

Gill, Fort Collins

Gill noted in his *American Alpine Journal* article that flying moves, lunges, swinging leaps, and moves where the climber had more or less to fling his body through the air from one hold to another, were not execrable mutations of good technique--as thought by many classical mountaineers. These methods could be disciplined and artistically executed. In addition, they were perfectly valid, as well as logical, techniques for a climber with a flair for acrobatics.

Yet Gill's true element was solitude, except for the times he would boulder with a partner (and even then he cherished the solitude of nature and sharing it with a friend). He liked to walk about in the woods or through mountain terrain and either avoided busy climbing areas or made himself unseen in such areas. He did not conform to mainstream perspectives but rather was drawn to the expression of his own inclinations in some solitary place that had obscure, indistinct-looking rocks or lost cliffs. Throughout the country, many small, steep surfaces of rock that mattered to no one else consumed him. His mind went to the lone, critical, microcrystal of rock that was the key to a single move. Yet a typical ten or fifteen-foot high Gill problem, one difficult enough for him to give it his private grading of "B2," would be less attainable for most climbers than the summit of Everest.

Gill, Fort Collins

The Mental Block, Fort Collins

Gill, Fort Collins

Gill in fact was beginning to be accorded the same respect as Walter Bonatti, Hermann Buhl, or Royal Robbins. His celebrity was derived from these very small rock climbs--boulders. From the Shawangunks in New York and the rocks of Devil's Lake, in Wisconsin, to more obscure areas of Alabama or Montana or Misourri, in South Dakota and a host of areas in Wyoming, and throughout Colorado, Gill left a mysterious presence that climbers local to each area could respect.

Gill at Devil's Lake, Wisconsin

The test for an aspiring climber was to see how well s/he could do to repeat a route that Gill had established.

Steve Wunsch writes about such a try:

Ever wanted to make an outrageous assertion and get away with it? Just pick the blankest side of a boulder or the most ridiculous looking overhang and say that a few years ago you saw John Gill walk by and climb it. Now if the individual you are trying to "sandbag" has had the privilege of visiting areas where Gill has climbed, the worst you're likely to meet in the way of skepticism is a wide-eyed "How?"

Kevin Bein was disarmingly well prepared for my query ("How?") and responded with a flourishing, carriage-road ballet amply narrated with talk of side-pulls, levers, and swing moves. He almost had me believing it until he had Gill jumping off from several feet above the overhang where Gill thought better of trying to mantel on a pile of sloping, wet leaves.

"Nobody would jump off from up there!" I said.

"He did. He down-climbed a move first, jumped off, then walked on down to the next problem."

Well, sandbagging is the name of the game in the Shawangunks. So while we were setting up the top-rope I half sensed that I was about to be taken for a ride, and I don't mean up. This supposed climb sported an overhang just as big and about as high as Doug's Roof (indeed it was the same roof but went over just a bit left, where there was no crack). The number of man-hours and roped falls which went into the freeing of Doug's Roof are an embarrassing matter of public record. If Kevin had tried this tale on me using anyone but Gill as its hero I'm sure I would have dismissed it instantly. But the mere mention of Gill's name evokes memories which seem to establish credence for the wildest of human aspirations. Didn't I try every Sunday one winter to do the left side of the Eliminator at Fort Collins? I eventually got the lunge on that climb down well enough to bloody my left hand consistently on the hold but not hang onto it. I've seen pictures of him doing it without a rope. Or being in the Needle's Eye parking lot digging into my pack for the compass (I never did need it on Ben Nevis) to see if that really was the Thimble's north face. It was. Or standing under the Red Cross Overhang in the Tetons after years of trying, listening to the drizzle in the forest (I'd never really gotten high enough for rain to matter), thinking of the first bouldering I did in the Tetons, years before, and a bright-eyed, young friend saying with awe, almost whispering, "Want to see a 5.13 climb?" I did.

All modesty aside, I began to realize that this overhang with the rope now dangling down past it might actually go, unbelievable as it had seemed only minutes before. I even fancied that, using slight modifications of Kevin's pantomime, I might do it. I had, however, made some miscalculations as to the sizes of, and distances between, each of the holds and was quickly swinging onto the rope, glad at least of my calculation that "nobody would jump off from up there." In fact I didn't get anywhere near the spot Gill jumped off from. Nor, to my satisfaction, did anyone else that day.

The Shawangunks of New York, Doug's Roof area

76

Keyhole, the Shawangunks

The Shawangunks, Brat-Gill Variation and Larsen's Problem

Gill's Route, the Shawangunks

The goals of such refinement, such esoteric intensity, included, for Gill, an increase in consciousness, a sharper, clearer reality, a feeling that he weighed a little bit less, a mental attitude that upon occasion inspired "a slight sensation of telekinesis" or in fact minutely perceivable levitation.

In 1969, I was sitting alone in a deserted Camp 4--the bouldering area of Yosemite. Pine needles were in my climbing shoes, and chalk that I had been rubbing on my fingers was in my hair. The boulders had worn me out after a couple hours of ascending them. A breeze blew through the lofty trees, and I gazed upward at surrounding walls of granite that rose thousands of feet. A waterfall roared in the distance. The Sierra scene, spring smells, sun, and the sky were telling me to look beyond the surface of life. I began to reflect upon bouldering, its loneliness, its challenges. In the hot afternoon, a drop of sweat in my palm became a crystalline image of John Gill. He was encouraging me to laugh at myself, because I was too serious. I felt the intrigue of a man whose name was blowing softly through the forests of the Grand Tetons, the South Dakota Needles, Colorado, and many areas. I thought of his gentleness, an individual who was kind and who had a warm, astute sense of humor. I felt that the ascents I now was doing on the boulders of Camp 4 spoke of what I had learned from someone whose skill was superior.

After returning to Colorado, I bouldered several times with Gill. On Flagstaff Mountain and in Eldorado Canyon, he did many of the hardest problems with ease. The competitive instinct in me was high, and I felt gratified when he was challenged by one or two of my creations, including a one-arm mantel problem, and my "Right Side of the Red Wall." In a little amphitheater of rock, he decided not to attempt a steep wall I had done that involved finger pebbles and had a dangerous landing. I viewed that route as my own mini-Thimble.

Ament, Right Side of the Red Wall,
Flagstaff Mountain, Boulder, Colorado

Gill took me to a bouldering area along the trail to Gem Lake, near Estes Park, and we pushed our limits again at Split Rocks. At Fort Collins, Gill came out to the cliffs with me but was injured and did not attempt to climb. During the early '70s, the somewhat violent and supremely powerful expression of climbing that was Gill's had its physical price. A kind of "tennis elbow" that he renamed "climber's elbow" was plaguing him. The extent and seriousness of it were unknown, and both arms were affected, forcing him to quit climbing altogether until he was healed.

To relieve the tensions of school work and for some physical exercise, he hiked up and down the hills around Horse Tooth Reservoir. Climbing could be enjoyed vicariously, by accompanying Rich Borgman, or me, up to the bouldering of Horse Tooth. John belayed or acted as coach. He took me to a forest of hidden boulders west of Horse Tooth Reservoir where routes awaited exploration, and I pioneered a red, overhanging wall he gave me-- since it would have been his. I was in my best physical shape ever, and Gill, although depressed about his elbow, seemed inspired. The frustrations of his injury seemed to diminish with just the thought of climbing.

As I climbed alone on Flagstaff many evenings in the late '60s at the peak of my ability, often with the boulders all to myself, I experienced a few proud, inspired, invincible, moments. I had no idea, however, how momentary my time in the light was to be. As Gill began to heal and return to climbing, a badly torn tendon in the middle finger of my left hand and a deep injury of my right shoulder made the curtain more or less close on my personal hopes-- except to be able to climb the classic longer routes I most enjoyed in Eldorado or around Boulder. Climbers, such as I, would come and go, but Gill seemed to remain--as the standard.

When John started climbing again, after his elbows began to heal, he was so weak that he could not do five consecutive two-arm pullups. A few friends wondered if the days of his bouldering strong were finished.

After difficult months of using his mind as an instrument of healing and wondering if he would ever climb hard again, he entered the game with a new attitude. He would warm up more carefully and for longer periods before attempting anything difficult. He was a little more picky as to choice of routes. And he forcibly controlled the impulse to keep at a problem beyond the familiar point of diminishing returns.

Bob Williams speaks of his initial impressions of Gill:

One look at Smith Overhang on Flagstaff in 1969, and I was hooked. Coming from the east with little climbing experience, I had never seen anything that difficult. My dreams were of El Cap, but my true love of bouldering had just begun. Like most climbers, I tried moves statically. Unlike most climbers, I didn't have enough strength. It soon became obvious that Smith's would require lunging, and since I saw even good climbers lunging now and then, I was quick to accept it as semi-legitimate technique. Besides, I really wanted to climb that overhanging piece of rock. I liked dynamic moves, because they allowed me to keep pace with my contemporaries. In my case, however, I overdid it, and I think many people frowned on my style--it wasn't pretty.

Encouraged by Dave Rearick, I decided to seek out John Gill-- the undisputed master of dynamic bouldering. I ventured to Fort Collins, hoping to find problems that could only be done with dynamic moves. John and Rich Borgman gave me the grand tour, wonderful problems on wonderful rock. Still, I wasn't prepared for what I saw there. At the Right Eliminator, John poised himself at the base with one hand casually placed on a small hold, then hopped from the ground to a good hold high on the route. The Mental Block provided more of these controlled jumps from the ground. It bothered me that he started so many problems this way, no matter that they were quite hard to do. I thought, "This can't be fair. Why avoid the problem by jumping past it?" Unconcerned with any rules committee, John played by his own rules. He did these jumps simply because they were aesthetically pleasing to him. He was, of course, quite capable of very difficult moves both from the ground and well above it. I never became comfortable with this technique, even to this day. At Fort Collins, however, I found more than a mentor. I found my savior.

Lora and John stayed in Fort Collins until 1971. She completed a bachelor's degree in mathematics at Colorado State University, graduating at the same time Gill earned his Ph.D. John was offered a position as assistant professor of mathematics at the University of Southern Colorado, and he, Lora, and Pam moved to Pueblo. In the draws and foothills around Pueblo, John's mental divining rod quickly located excellent bouldering possibilities.

Before long, Gill had pioneered many routes around Pueblo of an extremely advanced level.

The Ripper Traverse, Pueblo, Colorado

84

Solo bouldering with self-belay rig, Pueblo, Colorado, mid-'70s

Even having slowed the pace of his bouldering, Gill was far from incapacitated. He met Warren Banks at this time who became a good friend and bouldering companion.

Warren describes their relationship:

My initial contact with John Gill was an anxious phone call that I made after receiving information from my Colorado Springs friend Steve Cheney that John was living in Pueblo. John was very cordial and receptive to my expressed interest in climbing with him. Within a week, he invited me to travel with him and his family to Boulder (Flagstaff Mountain) for the day. That day at Flagstaff served not only to permanently redirect my perspective on climbing but also marked the beginning of what would evolve into a very valued friendship.

During the next couple of years (1971-72), I gratefully and enthusiastically followed John through southern Colorado cactus, scrub oak, and junipers, from one bouldering area to another. John discovered, as well as established, more areas and routes than I would have believed existed in the foothills and canyons in the Pueblo vicinity. Even more incomprehensible is John's ability to ascend these seemingly unclimbable gems once he has located them. Many of the ethereal feats that John accomplished in my presence were the first ascents of what are now considered among the "classic" front-range test pieces (Ripper Traverse, Little Overhang, the Fatted Calf problems, etc.).

Gill on the Fatted Calf, Pueblo

John also introduced me to a number of other climbing areas, such as Veedauwoo and Horse Tooth Reservoir, and to several accomplished, genuinely talented climbers, such as Rich Borgman, Bob Williams, and Pat Ament. The opportunities that John provided me to climb in diverse areas with world-class talent greatly impacted both my ability and motivation. I tend to view my tenure with John as a gift that very few are fortunate enough to receive. While I have experienced the good fortune of climbing with a number of exceptional partners over the last twenty years, none has been more influential to my climbing or personal life than John Gill!

> **Much has been said, or written, about John's impeccable character. I can only reiterate--he is an absolutely model human being. For an individual to be so nonchalant, particularly in light of so much accomplishment--not only in climbing but also in career and personal life--is truly remarkable.**

After two years in Pueblo, Lora and John decided to divorce--agreeing that love was gone. Lora needed to develop her own potential if she ever was going to. It was an uncomplicated divorce, or reasonably so, as such matters go. They filled out the forms themselves, not bothering with an attorney. One of the agreements of the divorce settlement was that, since Lora's future was uncertain, John would keep Pam, even though Lora dearly loved her daughter. Lora wanted to go back to school and wanted to be able to move around from job to job. She lived in Pueblo for awhile, attending school at the junior college and also at U.S.C. She lived across town, and Pam divided her time between her mother and father. Then Lora moved to Trinidad, Colorado. She worked there for several months, and John put Pam on a bus on weekends. Eventually Lora moved to New York, remarried, and came to work as a computer analyst.

At least one climbing friend of John's speculated that Lora had adopted the thinking of a "liberated woman" at which moment the fate of their marriage was sealed. Reflecting in a letter to me, however, Gill stated:

> *"I accept a large part of the responsibility for the failure of our marriage. I was too self-centered, too focused on teaching, and mathematics, and climbing. Not sensitive to her needs. Made career decisions that took us to places having few opportunities for her. I feel guilty about not being a better father to Pam, although I am very proud of her."*

One of John's happiest memories is of telling Pam a long adventure story, a continuing saga with a new chapter each evening before bedtime, during the year or so they lived alone. She and he backpacked into the Wind River range in Wyoming and fished for several days, shortly before John and Lora separated.

John and Pam continued to live in the house that Lora and he had purchased in the Belmont area of Pueblo, below the college.

Dorothy Boggs was a student in one of his intermediate algebra classes in 1973, working at the time toward a respiratory therapy degree. They began dating and were married in Pueblo in 1974. Dorothy had a son, Chris, who was fourteen, and a daughter, Susan, who was eleven. Pam at the time was nine. John sold his house in Belmont, and Pam and he moved up to Dorothy's house in Colorado Springs. She had been commuting from Colorado Springs, and they lived there for a month while looking around Pueblo for a place of their own. They found an old, attractive house on Third Avenue, a small, two-story dwelling built around the turn of the century. It seemed about the right price, had a certain charm, including pecan floors, and looked as though it would provide enough room for everyone. They sold Dorothy's house and moved into the Third Avenue home where they would stay for eleven years.

In the middle of winter, 1975, I bouldered with Gill west of Pueblo and found that indeed his injuries were not bothering him if they still existed at all. While acutely aware of the possibility of re-injury, he climbed brilliantly. I brought with me a small 16-millimeter movie camera with black-and-white film. The camera didn't work properly, would shut off with Gill frozen in mid-flight at the climactic move, but provided a few laughs and ultimately enough footage to make a short, very rough, collector-item film. The most astonishing sequence captured was a route on "The Fatted Calf" boulder. This involved a dynamic move where he threw himself outward and upward, starting off difficult holds under an overhang, and where he then became completely detached from the rock for an instant before grabbing with one hand (at the limit of his reach) a sloping hold at the lip of the overhang. Great stress then tested his hand's friction on the lip as his body swung free from under the overhang. A one-arm pull began the final process of moving over the actual lip.

Free aerial move on the Fatted Calf boulder, Pueblo

One ability of Gill's was to seek out routes that called forth something of the unique powers he possessed, routes that perfectly fit his height and physiology and particular strengths.

Bob Candelaria summarizes an encounter with Gill:

> **On the way to one of Gill's bouldering sites, I see that more than the mere physical effort of climbing is required. It takes a gift to actually locate these areas. Observing Gill in profile driving his Volkswagen bus, I imagine his fingers being, in actuality, witching sticks for locating boulders. Gill, Ament, and I arrive at an amphitheater of rock where the ballet is to begin. John's dog, a red, half-Irish Setter named Gallo, scruffles up the backside of the amphitheater and races along the rim of the cliffs, then finds a pool of**

mud and water in which to play. Standing at the base of the Ripper Traverse, Gill breathes in gasps. He does not touch the rock, nor does he simply climb it. He in essence transcends the route. He is across it.

Gill, Pueblo

Visiting the Needles in '75, John was ascending a one hundred-foot spire a short distance from the Needle's Eye parking lot on a humid summer afternoon. In his words:

> *"I found myself pathetically grappling with slippery quartz crystals, patiently belayed by my wife, Dorothy. As I turned a corner halfway up the spire, I was spotted by two huge beer-drinking motorcyclists, clothed in what appeared to be uniforms of the Rumanian Iron Guard. As they sat on the hood of the car of a petrified tourist, whose*

casual acquaintance they had just formed, they yelled to me, 'Get the hell off that rock!' With sweat pouring into my eyes and a dismal climbing performance jading my thoughts, I promptly shouted back, 'Come get me!' A moment of tense silence gripped the Black Hills. Automobile traffic came to a halt, and touring families exchanged worried looks as they quickly rolled up their windows, locked their doors, and stuffed their small children into the back seats. The two motorcyclists focused their attention on me, with a look that was a perfect blend of cruelty and serendipitous pleasure. One of them effortlessly and with quiet arrogance pulled a beer can apart. The pieces tinkled to the ground. Remembering Dorothy on the ground, I quickly began mental calculations of distance and rappelling and running speed.

"Suddenly the two cyclists shook their heads, and their expressions changed to (of all things) bland indifference. They slid off the hood onto their Harleys and roared off with only the quickest glance at the daily and predictable casualty that unfailingly warmed the hearts of climbers: the Greyhound tour bus, as usual, had jammed against the rock and become stuck in the Needle's Eye tunnel, shedding its glassy tinsel to the satisfaction of children and climbers alike.

"My spirits bolstered by these fortuitous developments, I shouted around the corner of the spire to my belayer, 'It's OK Dorothy, they've gone,' only to hear her reply coming from a quarter mile away, 'That's good. I'll see you at the campground.'"

In January, 1976, after a spaghetti dinner, Gill and I sat at the kitchen table of his house in Pueblo. We talked climbing for a couple of hours, with a tape recorder running, then retired to the living room and continued the discussion until the recorder shut off. We noticed later that some of our comments seemed downright spaghetti-bloated. It was a "fireside chat" under the auspices of gathering information for a possible film. Gill's sense of humor, honesty, insight, and self-effacing perceptions were a kind of one-finger pullup of humility. He was setting the standards in more ways than one.

The following are a few of his comments from that interview:

"I guess I've been very fortunate. The people that have bouldered with any degree of seriousness, with whom I have been acquainted, have all developed beautifully. I've always managed to pick something up from them, some little bit of technique, some form, style, things that are difficult to put your fingers on. It has always been an educational experience for me when I go out with a young climber who is quite good.

"I wouldn't say that I take a climber and mold him. These people, practically all of them, have an excellent reservoir of raw talent.

"I'm never quite sure what kind of day I'm going to have. Sometimes when I hit it, as the expression goes, I do extremely well. On other occasions, I've been known to do very poorly on just mediocre rock.

"I like bouldering sessions where you can afford to laugh at yourself and laugh at each other. I'll have to admit that, in some instances in the past eight or ten years, I have felt a bit like the classical, old, western gunfighter who is always being goaded into a shoot-out on Main Street.

"I'd rather go out with a friend, an acquaintance with whom I can relax a little, as opposed to someone to whom I must prove my absurdly impractical abilities all over again.

"My climbing philosophy has more or less stabilized at this point in life. I enjoy very competitive bouldering on occasion, not always. I get quite a bit of satisfaction out of re-climbing routes that I have established. I've never felt compelled to do something that somebody else has done.

"From time to time I've been locked in the grips of a consuming passion for this route or that. But these have been periods of short duration. I don't hold a grudge against a nemesis. I've always enjoyed hiking. That's been an entirely separate activity for me within the mountain

realm. When I go hiking, I usually don't even think about bouldering. I can walk beneath a beautiful boulder, and it will catch my eye just for a moment. I'd rather look at the flowers, the trees, the birds.

"At the Hagermeister boulders, it must have been in the very early 1960's, I drove up for a session of bouldering, got out of the car, took my shoes and chalk, walked over to the standard slab route, and sat down. When I picked up my shoes to put them on, there was a twenty-dollar bill lying on the ground. So I put my street shoes back on, put the twenty-dollar bill in my pocket, took my shoes and chalk, went back to the car, and drove to town (Estes Park). And that was probably the most enjoyable bouldering session I've ever had.

"A good bouldering route is not one where the sequence of holds is perfectly obvious. It should be difficult to discover the correct sequence, and it should be difficult to execute the sequence. I do mathematical research, and you might be surprised by the very close parallel that exists between the two pursuits--one, apparently purely intellectual, the other apparently purely physical. In both instances, a person stands more or less at a frontier. It is enlightening to follow the proof of an established theorem, but far more satisfying to discover a new theorem. It is a creative enterprise, and I do not believe in painting a picture by numbers. One takes a blank canvas and does something original.

Acrobat Overhang, on Castle Rock, west
of Boulder, Colorado, in the early '60s

*"In both bouldering and mathematics, you stand
upon the threshold of something new, something that
requires not only brute force (whether it be physical or
intellectual force) but a certain insight, a certain quantum
jump from point to point. I don't mean making a physical
jump, although sometimes that helps! Something is there
that can be created, possibly, if one uses insight, intuition,
etc., in order to make this quantum jump. One discovers
that the bouldering route can be accomplished not by
looking at each minute hold, foot by foot, but by looking at
the overall route. One gets an instinctive feeling that it can
be done and then starts looking closely for and at holds.
You usually find that they are there.*

*"In bouldering, you're concerned as much--if not
more--with form, style, elegance, and route difficulty as
you are with getting to the top. There are all sorts of routes*

that don't end on the tops of boulders. Traverses, for example. There are exceptional climbs that go part way up a cliff. You run into a blank wall, jump off, and that's the end of the bouldering problem. I've spoken with mountaineers about this sort of thing. It's usually difficult for them to adjust to a feeling for the small when they've been so concerned with the large. One little epigram that Chouinard once applied to bouldering was, 'Instant suffering.' I'll agree. It's as if you take a lengthy climb and squeeze it down into one or two moves. To compensate for decreased length, you increase the difficulty.

"Perhaps with an excellent mental attitude. you not only integrate your moves better but this in turn induces a telekinesis to levitate you slightly, even if it is only taking off a few ounces. A few ounces can make a tremendous difference.

"I feel that the bond of friendship, the roped team, may be a manufacturer as well as a transmitter of psychic energy."

Yvon Chouinard, in a taped conversation in Yosemite in the mid-'70s, added to Gill's thoughts:

Climbing is still in a stage of pure physical movement, and the next step is going to be mind control. I think Gill has already gone into that, from watching him prepare for a boulder even in the late '50s. I would walk up to a boulder and just do it. He would sit below a route, do his little breathing exercises, and get his mind prepared, like a weight lifter walking up to a set of weights, getting his mind calmed down and his body ready to go. You're going to have to use meditation and Yoga to be able to get up some of the new climbs, because pure physical strength and technique are not going to be enough. You're going to have to climb as if you're two feet off the ground. I think it's going to be Zen and the art of rock climbing.

That's what the book The Inner Game of Tennis is all about. They've taken people who are learning tennis, and one group goes out and plays every day for two weeks while another group just sits down, meditates, thinks about improving, thinks about how they're going to swing the racket, getting it all set in their minds, and the group that concentrates on it rather than plays becomes more skillful. Climbing is going to be the same way. You know, you can go out one day and play pool, and you're just an average player, but you simply look at the balls and know they're going to sink in the pockets. You grab the cue, you don't even think, then you run the whole table. You try to do it another day, and you can't. Why does that happen? When it gets to the point where we can, at will, conjure up these exceptional days, there'll be some incredible things occurring.

I asked Gill in our fireside interview what advice he would give to climbers, with regard to training. The following are a few comments he offered.

"I firmly believe that most people who wish to pursue bouldering can really benefit from formal gymnastics: rope climbing, still-rings, parallel bars, some high-bar, free exercise.... I have personally never used weights for training except to do a one-arm pullup with twenty to thirty pounds in the other hand.

One-arm pullup with weights

"What's worked best for me has been a combination of actual bouldering and certain forms of gymnastics. The weakest link between the climber and the rock is the fingers. Unfortunately, finger strength is probably the most difficult to develop and keep. It is the first to go with increased age. There are exercises that I have used to develop my fingers--fingertip chins on doorjambs and, ultimately, one-arm chins on the first joint of the fingers. This tends to develop power more than stamina. In most instances, a boulderer is concerned with a sudden burst of power, as opposed to long-term stamina, but not always. The sort of strength one develops when working on the still rings seems to carry over to climbing. It gives you a certain amount of poise under stress, on overhangs for example. I was able to do butterfly mounts on the rings moderately easily and an iron cross. I did an inverted cross on occasion."

Gill said that to see good bouldering was to see a graceful display of athletic ability, the same type of precision apparent in good dance, the same balance, coordination, and strength. He added that bouldering was therapeutic.

Gill, the Needles of South Dakota

Soloing the Final Exam on Castle Rock, near Boulder, Colorado, early '60s

At Split Rocks, Colorado

Using my "interview" with Gill, I wrote a short book about him without his knowing I was doing so until I presented him with the final draft. It was a "portrait," as I called it. At a small author-publisher signing celebration, the cork of a champagne bottle fired off and hit the ceiling when Gill's name was mentioned. Everyone took this to be a message that the book would be a hit. The book sold out almost instantly, a tribute to the respect climbers had for Gill.

As David Breashears said one day, "Gill is the true spiritual climber from whom we can all learn."

I climbed with John a number of times in Pueblo. In "Lost Canyon," a river-gully hidden in the badlands east of Pueblo and filled with blocks of Dakota sandstone, I formulated a static variation of a dynamic route he had created. He was pleased with my solution, an application of difficult stemming techniques, and later reported to me that other of his friends who tried the problem could do the dynamic variation but not my static one. All of those climbers had stronger biceps than I. It felt good now and then to find my own abilities, those that were who I was as an individual, yet my injured finger and shoulder, combined with an increased loss of desire for training and the genetic disposition to put on the buxom pounds of my great grandmothers, prevented me from being an ultimate competitor for either Gill or for myself. Our friendship, fortunately, was not contingent upon ability, and we amused ourselves on whatever difficulty matched the mood.

Gill in Lost Canyon, Pueblo

Yet there were always demonstrations he would make of some preposterous configuration of rock. He gave me a tour of "buildering" problems at the university, at one point clamping a square corner (rib) of slick cement and ascending it. He showed me other routes inside the building that could be done when the students were gone. We practiced wire-walking on slack chains around the campus.

Buildering a cement rib on the University of
Southern Colorado campus

Another afternoon, we illegally traversed a man-made, stone
wall above an open polar bear pit at the Pueblo Municipal Zoo
where my old gymnastic abilities seemed suddenly to come alive.
They had not been forgotten altogether--as I began to imagine the
consequences of a fall!

West of Pueblo, Gill found several six to eight hundred-foot
granite buttresses on the side of a steep, wooded hillside. These
"Quiet Towers," as he called them, appealed to him because they
were broken by large ledges, or tiers, lending less of a sheer

appearance and more of a friendly one. Here Gill could move from tier to tier up pinkish-white granite, enjoy the sky, and explore "the still faces of nature." In the mid-'70s, I followed him up one of these long, relatively easy solo climbs. At a moderately difficult section where I preferred to have a belay, he pulled a short, fifty-foot rope from his waist-pack and lowered an end of it to me. It appeared to be clothesline rope. When I asked if it was any good, he assured me, "I just bought it at K-Mart the other day."

Gill formed good friendships with many outstanding boulderers, including Curt Shannon, Bob Murray, Lew Hoffman, Bob D'Antonio, Warren Banks, Chris Jones, and Bob Williams.

Bob Williams climbing Gill's Juggernaut route in Lost Canyon, Pueblo

Jim Holloway was an especially stunning bouldering talent whose company Gill esteemed. "The fabulous Holloway," as Gill referred to him, reminisces:

> I had been climbing and bouldering for several years when Bob Williams invited me to go with him and John Gill in Pueblo. I was eighteen years old, and I was not going to miss this for anything. When we arrived at John's house, he showed us his set of rings in the backyard. After seeing front levers, handstands, etc., the kind of gymnastic moves you usually only see on television, I decided not to humiliate myself by attempting a two-arm hang, deadman's swing, or such. I was going to save all the strength I had.
>
> We took John's car to the bouldering area. I even got to ride "shotgun"--wow! Maybe Bob let me sit up front so that I would see the small, gold name-plate in the dashboard that said: This car made especially for John Gill (no joke). I was impressed.
>
> I learned a lot that day about dynamic moves, about doing them smoothly and in control. I was very interested in learning and in pushing my own limits. Now that I had seen this dynamic style done so flawlessly by John, I was hooked.
>
> Now--years later--having travelled to many of the areas across the U.S.A. that John bouldered at in the 1960's, I have learned more from his remarkable routes. Not only do they take great ability and knowledge but a certain awareness--all combined in a special way. I am grateful to have bouldered with John Gill. He has been the greatest inspiration in my bouldering, as I know he is to boulderers everywhere.

Jim Holloway

In and around bouldering, Gill continued to find time for long solos that had "invigorating" exposure. These involved no gear except for chalk and climbing shoes. By keeping levels of difficulty down, he was able to concentrate more on the pursuit of discovery in a classic mountaineering sense. Yet from moment to moment, a brief and real rock climbing challenge might appear. In an article in *The Climbing Art* magazine, he wrote how one such solo on these high buttresses ended with an overhang and some climbing of a very exhilarating character. He wrote how he loitered on a face of rock above the overhang and played for a moment to convince himself that he "really could have done some alarmingly difficult climbing" had he wanted to.

Competition with his younger friends was a motivating factor in bouldering but played virtually no role in these longer, very private solo climbs. They fulfilled the simple ecstasy of being in the mountains and allowed him to move and flow and to enjoy climbing on his own terms, without the underlying sense of rules or expectations that often crept in during bouldering.

A very tall Scott Blunk spent part of the summer of 1979 bouldering with Gill and shares a few impressions of that time:

> It had been a great bouldering year for me: I did second ascents of some very hard routes at Horsetooth, climbed the Red Cross problems in the Tetons, and repeated most of the Gill routes in the Needles, including the Thimble via top-rope. That was all accomplished in the spring, so I was feeling mighty proud of myself by the time I moved down to Pueblo. I spent the summer there doing an internship at the State Hospital. I worked on a psychiatric ward, and it was a pretty crazy place--some people hallucinating about snakes, others lurking fearfully in corners, while still others nursed delusions of grandeur. I fit right into the latter category with my firm belief that I was the best boulderer in the world.
>
> Of course I looked up Gill right away, and off we went. We toured the beautiful sandstone outcrops around Pueblo, each week visiting a new area. John put up with my youthful enthusiasm and impatience and, by way of example, taught me two important lessons about bouldering.
>
> He had one very powerful problem west of town where he hardly used his feet. He just cranked one-arms all the way up this bulging wall. I jumped on it immediately, thinking, "Aha! Here's another coup for my war bag!" I failed miserably. Couldn't even do it using my feet. I went back to the hospital feeling lower than the imaginary snakes. And the worst thing about it was that Gill hadn't gloated over my failure at all. He just said that it was a neat route, one

that he liked to do. That puzzled me, for I surely would have crowed over someone else's failure.

The second lesson was just as puzzling. I had found an obscure little variant on the Penny Ante Boulder, something that I felt utterly compelled to do. After a lot of work, I succeeded. It turned out to be a long lunge on rather marginal holds. Gill tried it a couple of times without success, offered some praise for its difficulty, then apparently forgot about it. I was stunned. Here was a route in his home territory, and he didn't CARE?! I wondered if I should talk with a psychiatrist about this. Didn't you have to repeat a route just because it was hard?

It took me awhile (years in fact) to figure out that bouldering is a very personal thing, that John climbed to satisfy his inner self rather than to satiate external expectations. Now that more than a decade has gone by, I can look back and smile at the struggles of an impetuous youth and, more importantly, remember a great summer's bouldering with John Gill.

Gill spoke to me of a mystical reality that, as he described, was "an extension of the hypnagogic state." He suggested that certain exertions in bouldering occasionally produced an apparent separation of "I-consciousness" and physical body, similar to how the mind of a long-distance runner seemed to soar above the automaton-like running form.

The idea of the metaphysical in climbing would be the subject of bemused speculation, were it not advanced by Gill. The reality of Gill's experiences hit home as you watched him climb, and the credibility of what he said grew if you were one of his bouldering friends and became acquainted with his honesty and humility. Gill very obviously was not some kind of weird recluse with delusions, rather a respected mathematician, very much a realist.

These were mystical perceptions in part inspired by his practice of "the art of Dreaming," as described in Carlos Castenedas' fictional works on Don Juan. Gill had upon occasion slipped into an alternate world. In utter solitude while ascending a steep tower in one of his climbing sanctuaries, he once had the ineffable experience of merging with and re-emerging from the yellowish and polished surface of the granite. Experiences such as these were "entirely the consequences of meditative practices," for he had never used psychedelic drugs.

In contrast to such "removed," or "mystical," states, and moments of separation from climbing, Gill appreciated equally--if not more--the pleasure of "an intense realization OF the experience," the mind "saturated with kinaesthetic awareness," states of reality defined by grace and precision and "momentum." As sequences on gymnastics apparatus were flavored by dynamics or by momentum, so could such values be added to the repertoire of the rock climber. In an essay on the subject of advanced dynamic climbing, Gill invited readers to "visualize a boulderer passing through two or more sequential moves," propelled upward by "the momentum from the first dynamic surge." Gill seemed fond of the phrase "kinaesthetic awareness," meaning perhaps "self-realization," a turning inward where all realms--sensory, mental, athletic, artistic, intellectual, mystical, spiritual, and aesthetic--united.

He climbed with inner quiet mingled with the concentration of artistic gymnastics, intimately involved with the beauty of nature. He knew the terrain in general, felt the breezes in the trees, or the quiet of the hills. Climbing had, after all, to do with the aesthetic qualities of the mountains, with sensuous exploration, as much as it did with the exhilaration of ascending rock. Just as the rock had its varied look and feel and inspired its own type of clarity, so did surrounding nature stimulate the mental creativity of perception and charge the electrical energies of the mind.

With its ongoing bursts of vision, climbing had, for Gill, the potential of being ever-fulfilling.

John saw a doctor after a brief experience with tachycardia and was informed that he was "out of shape." He was in fact very much in shape muscularly, but the brief surges of power in bouldering were insufficient to maintain cardiovascular conditioning. He adjusted his exercise to include more walking, hiking, kicking a soccer ball in a nearby park, and working out on a Nordic track.

Gill at Veedauwoo, Wyoming, late '60s

He and Dorothy built a lovely but modest solar home isolated in the prairie of Pueblo West, not far from the foot of the Rockies.

In 1986, Gill gave two delightful, well-received talks, first in March of 1986 as a guest speaker at the bi-annual national conference of the British Mountaineering Council in Buxton, England, and then in December at the annual American Alpine Club meeting in Denver. I was fortunate to be able to go with him and Dorothy to England where the British audience sat admiringly and listened to the bouldering stories and the philosophies that Gill presented in his humble, witty, but slightly verbose, academic style.

Pat Ament and John and Dorthy Gill, in Buxton, England, 1986

At an English indoor climbing wall, Gill demonstrated his abilities unexpectedly by casually approaching an overhang and doing a new route up it that involved an impressive aerial move. Witnesses to this short moment were dumbfounded, having not seen a person fly upward with such ease over such small holds. Talk of the route spread instantly through England, although no one could remember exactly the holds or the sequence Gill used.

At the Alpine Club meeting in Denver, he put a statement by writer Somerset Maugham into the climbing vernacular: "There are three rules that will enable a climber to succeed at any pitch. Unfortunately, no one knows what they are." Gill also stated that he was "never one to be intimidated by the absence of danger."

That summer of '86, Patrick Edlinger, one of France's top competitive climbers, visited Boulder and asked me to show him the Gill test pieces at Fort Collins. After this visit to Fort Collins, it seemed clear to me that Gill's bouldering throughout the 1970's had not been surpassed or even equalled as yet by the star climbers of the '80s.

John returned in July of 1987, at the age of fifty, to the Tetons for a rendezvous with those old bouldering problems that were his first personal test pieces. His performance on the dynamic route on Red Cross Rock was disappointing. He climbed many other routes, however, that he had established nearly thirty years earlier. Reaching the small hold at the lip of Red Cross, he was unable to continue over the top.

Gill, Red Cross direct north overhang, photo by Alicia Jones

Not many other climbers had done the route, although a few through the years had claimed success by an easier method created when a flake broke and left a large, comfortable fingertip hold. Gill knew the difference between that and the true problem. It was a sad testament that a key feldspar crystal on his route "The Scab," in the Needles, also had been altered by someone (in 1980) and made more usable.

Chris Jones, a very strong, remarkable boulderer whose philosophies seemed to Gill to be especially compatible with his own, met Gill in the Tetons on this return visit and, this same afternoon at Red Cross Rock, after an energetic struggle, succeeded at the route using the original Gill formula.

Although Gill's experience went far beyond ordinary recreational rock climbing, recreation and play were rarely absent. He was equally drawn to very easy rock where he was able to move meditatively. Difficulty, it was apparent to his friends, played only a partial role in his attachment to the sport. Clearly the experience was a transcendent one, whether engaged in the challenge of an almost impossible overhang or scrambling up an easy slant.

Part of that transcendence has been the lighthearted spirit that is one of the genteel qualities of Gill. He is absolutely free of rudeness or vulgarity. He is acutely observant, wise, and possesses a fine inner being. His is a generosity that lies at the heart of all high, human experience. Admitting with delightful humor his particular quirks and specialization, he never fails to credit friends with every inch of height that they earn, his humility as spectacular as his climbing moves.

In October of 1987, at the age of fifty, Gill was bouldering in surprisingly good form. He was heartened to experience a physical renewal. He could still do front levers and one-arm, fingertip pullups.

Gill, Pueblo, photo by Dorothy Gill

A high variation of the Ripper Traverse, Pueblo, photo by Dorothy Gill

Yet he also admitted that taking his golden retriever Dusty for a stroll across the quiet prairie, dining out with friends, or writing about climbing instead of doing it were becoming increasingly attractive.

A difficult dynamic route in Little Owl Canyon, Pueblo

In an attempt to make his tenth or so ascent of the "Micro-Shield," a short, severe problem at that time unrepeated by others on granite near his home in Pueblo, his foot slipped from a 2mm hold. As his weight came suddenly onto his extended right arm, the bicep was torn from the bone at the elbow joint. Aside from the pain, there was the gruesome effect of the bicep more or less "rolling" up to his shoulder under the skin of his arm.

Gill on the Micro-Shield, Pueblo

The surgeon who successfully re-attached the muscle speculated that the muscle had probably been held in place for years by little more than scar tissue and that the other arm could very well go in the same manner--if Gill was not careful.

After months of recovery and with a great deal of effort (he designed his own therapy), John was able to begin a few moderate exercises. He decided, however, that he would never attempt aerobatic, or dynamic, climbing again.

Any number of climbers visited Gill in Pueblo, however, and reported that he was a formidable climber even with the new preventive care that he applied to each route. A year and a half after his injury, he could again do a one-arm pullup with his injured (right) arm.

Except for a periodic return to the boulders "to assess the damage," Gill's climbing more and more returned to its origins-- found in the unpretentiousness of long, usually moderate solo ascents in solitude, the way he had found adventure as a young man. His passion for extreme bouldering disappeared quickly. There was no desire to repeat the experience of a detached bicep, or otherwise destroy himself in one explosive dynamic move. Excellent solace and considerable challenge could be found in these longer, exploratory solos.

He returned again to the Tetons in July of '89, to his old haunt of soaring, gray peaks where there were lakes and where he could encounter "a veritable jungle of large, leafy green plants rioting among huge Douglas-fir and ponderosa pine." Clouds circled the mountains and sent shadows across meadows of lupine. Rock rose precipitously into clear Wyoming air.

Carrying only a couple of slings and a fifty-foot length of nylon rope purchased at K-Mart, he began up Delicate Arete--the long ridge he had made the first ascent of in 1958. He still remembered vividly his second ascent of the route, where he had found himself on a barren edge of rock on tiny holds while buffeted by strong winds--"so close to peeling," as he wrote in *The Climbing Art* magazine, "that reality itself lost its cohesion."

"I have had tense moments in former years, clinging like an ant while unpredictable, angry winds pulled and pushed--an eternity of several minutes. Is it possible that I did, in fact, slip from those minute footholds? Has all that has happened in the presumable intervening years been illusion, woven with blinding speed into my last corporeal moments? Am I destined to return now, slip through a fold in time and greet the angry slabs as they rush toward me?

"The body is cold, it wants action, so I set aside these curious reflections and get on with the dance. Thirty years experience should be safeguard enough....

"The first few raindrops land on the already slick, high-angle slabs, and my apprehension returns....

"I am at the base of the corner of the yellow wall.... All I see is vertical rock, a few small cracks, and unnerving exposure.... I climb rapidly for thirty feet or so and pause. Then in a brief moment of middle-aged abandonment, I follow a whim and step around the corner to the edge of the yellow wall.

"I am instantly appalled by my ill-conceived action. This is no good--really difficult, practically vertical terrain, terribly exposed. The smooth, yellow pegmatite is inches from my face, its tiny crystals shimmering with moisture. Barely breathing, I move to the right with infinite caution-- foot, then hand, foot, then hand. Finally I am secure once again on the modest corner, and I relax and contemplate this egregious lapse. I have always felt that spontaneity is essential in finding a path upon the rock that makes the spirit soar, but this brief experience points to the danger of a more capricious, almost senile behavior."

In the fall of '89, Gill found a bit of moderate, solitary climbing on the limestone cliffs of the Calanques, in southern France, while he attended a mathematics meeting at the French government's International Center for Mathematical Research on the Luminy Campus of the University of Marseilles. By following a short path from the huge, pink chateau set in the forest, he encountered the blue Mediterranean spread out beautifully.

In 1990, at the age of fifty-three, Gill returned again to the Tetons and with a "playful attitude" soloed a seven hundred-foot new climb up the east side of the south face of Satisfaction Buttress. As Life Savers dissolved in his mouth, he ascended at his own speed, along the route of his liking, losing himself in exploration, with an occasional moment of excitement and challenge. At the finish of the climb, he experienced a fulfillment that was "mildly religious." In his usual understatement, he wrote in an article that his personal metaphor for this sort of climbing was "making a mountain out of a molehill."

On other "scrambles" during this trip to the Tetons, he continued to find excitement--for example descending off one route, where he was forced to climb through a short waterfall on "slick, overhanging rock."

Gill gave the type of soloing he particularly enjoyed on higher rocks the name "menu climbing" and then refined that to "option-soloing"--whereas many potential lines exist, with frequent easy scrambling alternatives, and many branch points that allow for spontaneous decisions appropriate to a given moment.

In August of 1991, on another visit to the Tetons, an intended option-solo materialized into the more serious feel of "free-soloing." He found himself on smooth, water-polished granite, making a few "airy steps" high up on the third tier of Trinity Buttress. One can assume that it was Gill's tremendous skill that made the consequences of these events manageable.

In a short, present-tense memoir, he wrote of this ascent:

"I move across a boulder field and up a steep, grassy slope to a tiny cave hidden in the trees at the base of Trinity Buttress--a tiered cliff. After stowing my blue day-pack, I put on my climbing shoes, belt pack, and coiled rappel line, and move up around the left corner of the cave onto an exposed but undistinguished ridge. I scan the buttress above. My route will be devious--three large cliffs are separated in a complex fashion by huge ledges covered with trees and brush.

"The transition from scrambling to climbing, that moment when you first glance down and see rocks and grass far beneath the contours of your feet, induces a heightened perception and a subtle change in body chemistry. I feel more locked into the evolving matrix of the present and less prone to drift in time and place. I move up the arete, ascending several minor steps in an increasingly airy environment, frictioning over rounded corners. Easy terrain on my right--I could scramble, practically walk up there if I wish--steep cliffs on my left, long and exposed. That's where previous climbs have been made.

"I move into a thirty-foot dihedral with abundant holds and climb quickly upward, passing in astonishment what appears to be a fresh Charlet-Moser piton: is this to be a dream-like day in the twilight zone of a thirty-year distant past? Whatever the context, this is the first fun pitch of the day--no grass, dirt or shrubs, just clean, firm rock. Above, I enter a strange, chaotic realm of precipitous rock walls, steep grassy ledges, and towering evergreens, some leaning over the corners of vast overhangs, their roots groping blindly into space. Color is everywhere--in the texture of the rock and the brilliant green of the trees.

"I move up through this turbulent landscape, guided more by whimsy than strategy. I imagine myself in an ancient poem--a medieval fairy tale--as I scramble along vertiginous ledges and over short bulges of lichen-covered granite, across precariously steep dirt slopes on the very edge of concave palisades, until finally reaching a broad shelf guarded by stately firs, the sentries of time. Beautiful white and tan slabs of polished granite sweep upward from here, two hundred feet to the top of the second tier of cliffs, capped by an uneven but continuous overhang.

"I pause for a few moments, thinking that at the age of fifty-four my climbing career has come full circle. I have returned to the origins of spirit, found in the simplicity of my earliest and most naive ascents.

"With some apprehension, I scan the long line of the overhang above me until spotting an obvious break where exposed scrambling may carry me through. Tip-toeing now, up and across to the west on lovely, firm, and slightly sculptured rock, an occasional optional move of unnecessary difficulty to add spice to my adventure, and I am suddenly near the crest of the overhang. I sense the tingle of exposure as I move up an easy crack to a foot-wide ledge directly beneath an abrupt, ten-foot step. If I negotiate a couple of elementary moves now, with my hands above on slabby holds, I'll be up and through the barrier.

"As I balance on my exposed perch, I hear voices of a climbing party across the couloir on the southwest ridge of Storm Point--a half mile away. A female climber, assertive to the point of belligerence, is leading two good-

124

natured men up a series of granite slabs. Her instructions ring clearly through the canyon. Instinctively, I begin to move in the direction she indicates! I knew long ago that the tough, hard-man, thoroughly masculine image of climbing would eventually vanish. I didn't foresee the peculiar androgynous analogue that would evolve, however.

"My attention interrupted by this display, I step over the bulge--exaggerating a simple move in the process. A trivial distraction, yet my technique has been degraded. I move quickly up onto dirt and scree slopes leading to a large boulder sitting a few feet from the vertical immensity of white and yellowish granite that forms the last and most significant part of Trinity Buttress.

"It's not good that I lost my concentration for a moment on the pitch below. That's not the way to endure in this solitary and dangerous meditation, this slowly deliberate, vertical stroll on edges of hard granite reality. In soloing, the margins of safety are maximized by shutting out anything other than the immediate technical requirements of climbing.

"Time for a few Life Savers. After some deliberation, I decide to climb on the eastern part of the buttress wall on rock that rises with increasing angle to a prominent shelf two hundred feet up. To the west, the rock is vertical and has few if any comfortable resting places. From my philosophical perspective, it lacks the virtue of available relaxing sections where a middle-aged explorer can recharge.

"I move upward and to the left, following a diagonal seam toward a small, rectangular block perched high on a minor ridge. The face I ascend becomes vertical toward the end of the pitch, capped by a slight overhang, but the holds are large and climbing not difficult. I fully expect to find a simple way up the last twenty feet above the block to the shelf seen from below, but when I arrive at the block I am face to face with uniformly steep, smooth, yellowish rock of severe appearance and breathtaking exposure--far too risky for unroped exploration.

"To the right of the crest, however, I see a favorable pattern of holds. Amazing how one's perspective changes. A few seconds ago, while beneath this section, I dismissed the possibility of going straight up, due to the exposure and wickedly smooth nature of the rock. Now I see that a couple of elementary but airy moves on newly discovered ledges will take me up the remainder of the face.

"Several minutes of increasingly disciplined, tentative steps off the block, onto the rock above, then back onto the block bring me to the point where determination exceeds the sense of jeopardy, and I move up a steep dihedral for several feet. I step around a corner, stretching my right leg to reach a ledge that slopes away from me and down and is carved into the wall above a small overhang far above the trees. I would never attempt this unprotected move without the new technology of sticky rubber soles.

"A short scramble leads to the shelf. Without pause for rational planning--deplorable but typical behavior when I get wound up in this frenetic sport--I start up a high-angle crack that appears to terminate thirty feet above at a ten-foot vertical face--seemingly replete, from its rough facade, with abundant edges and providing an easy exit into dirt gullies above that are filled with scree and bordered by shrubs and trees. The climbing on the smooth stone quickly becomes harder, and I run out of horizontal holds. I must move continuously, stemming and cross-pressuring my way up an inside corner until I reach the small face. At last some sloping footholds and a good hold for one hand...a chance to secure and pause and suppress the niggling anxieties that threaten to disturb the smooth flow of climbing technique.

"Slightly out of balance and with considerable space beneath my toes, I can see no more holds above me. Feeling that I am at the end of my hypothetical rope, I search for a way to negotiate a few feet of intimidating rock without calling on bouldering skills that I have largely avoided using since my injury.

"I still my mind and press tiny sparks of apprehension into the subconscious and calm the viscera

and subdue the slight muscle tremor, and I am ready to receive instructions. And...yes...my body drifts a step to the right, above the emptiness, and I am now nearly below a ledge, and I find a handhold and a sloping foothold and step up and stand above this thing I have become part of.

"It is over, and I scramble the remaining few feet to the top.

"I lose the descent path on the bottom tier of cliffs and wander back and forth across the wilderness of overhanging walls and tree-covered shelves, following ledges that lead nowhere, traversing steep, dangerous, earthen slopes, rappelling three times, until I am down to the level of the cave and my blue pack. It is 4:30, and I am weary and hungry. This day has been a bit more than I expected. The difficulties were, I am certain, less than they seemed, but the continual probing of the unknown strains the eye and the nerve and leaves the mind unsettled, insecure in the subtle turbulence of an existential ripple."

Lew Hoffman met Gill on this trip to the Tetons and, in the following account, captures a little of the spirit of his friendship with Gill:

John and I had occasionally talked of coordinating summer Teton visits. August of '91 finally found us at Gros Ventre campground with hopeful agendas and a dubious weather pattern. After I returned from a mostly rainy, two-day alpine effort, I cooked a pre-arranged clam sauce spaghetti dinner and waited for John at the campground.

He drove up as the next wave of rain soaked Jackson Hole. We hunkered under my meager tarp and dined as John recounted his day's adventure--he'd hiked into the Tetons, bushwhacked up to a face he'd been considering for a few decades, free-soloed the route (unlisted in any guide) up and down, and beat the storm back to the valley floor.

At the Jenny Lake ranger cabin that August, the common, repeated wisdom was that alpine activity, especially new routes, had dropped sharply since the action was on the new "sport" crags south of Jackson and on recently bolted Blacktail Butte (lines Gill had free-soloed thirty years before). I guess sport is where and how one finds it.

Gill solo climbs at Blacktail Butte, Wyoming, late '50s

Occasionally I hear a good, apocryphal Gill story and relay the story to John who is always amused and ready with an honest denial or truthful retelling. Here are two mini-myths that come to mind.

In Colorado Springs, after inelegantly scratching my way up a Garden Of The Gods problem (a mighty step upward to the first foothold, followed by a crux pull upward off of smoothly-weathered tourist initials chiseled long ago into the boulder), a local climber informed me that John Gill had done the problem first try, using only his left arm. John later said he'd never bouldered in the Garden.

During a foray to the Black Hills in the late '70s, stories were told around a campfire. Pete Cleveland exploits and tales of extracurriculars at the "sex cave" were great, but I didn't nasal snort a swallow of beer until the inevitable Gill story. Not even rock-related, this one had a group of climbers relaxing in a Custer bar when John joined them. John demonstrated a balance training routine, presumably before quaffing too many brews, by tiptoeing across empty beer bottles arranged along the bar top!

While on a sandstone bouldering outing in the mid-'80s, John mentioned his rekindled interest in granite—Black Hills-style bouldering he'd found in the mountains west of Pueblo. Gill envisioned climbing a vertical, totally blank slab.

On a fall day about a month later, we visited a granite area. John led me on a circuit of Needles-quality boulders. At the circuit's end, John and I spied and started "one last new route," while his wife Dorothy broke out our picnic lunch. We'd nubbined up to a blank spot which we now protected with a top-rope. After a few personal dynamic efforts to span the blank (all of which ended with my swinging horizontally on the rope at John's eye level), he glided the gap statically with a surprising reach involving a step on a micro-edge and a two-fingered pull into a one-arm mantel. I call the route the "Stretcher," and I suppose no one has tried this hidden classic since.

Flashing the route left John elated and Dorothy and I impressed. After John downclimbed the backside of the boulder, Dorothy said he'd appeared to use a magical rubber arm to effect the stretch. John laughed and attributed the feat to the "mystical element" of climbing.

Gill soloed a couple of long routes near Estes Park, Colorado, this same summer. He found a "moderate" route up the six hundred-foot Sundance Buttress and later, with his good friend Chris Jones, a master boulderer, soloed a rock buttress of Twin Sisters. In the following treatise, Chris Jones describes a joint solo near Pueblo and reflects about Gill:

"Now, around this corner there is more exposure. It gives me a different feeling." I looked across to the corner, and the several hundred feet of exposure below it, and thought to myself, "Hmm...yes, John, I can believe that it does." No doubt John was going to be feeling a heightened sense of elation when soloing this next section. No doubt this next section was going to give me a different feeling as well--heightened fear most likely.

John and I were unroped about half-way up one of his favorite soloing rocks, a two-tiered, 600-foot buttress in the mountains west of

Pueblo. Despite my apprehension, I was glad to be here with John and that he was sharing this experience with me.

Actually, he was sharing more than the experience of simply climbing a route without a rope. John has found for himself, and was teaching me, a novel variant of the unroped game. I will attempt to recount the lesson.

The idea is not simply to ascend, but to have the freedom to ascend in precisely the way that feels right at the moment. The selection of what is to be climbed is very important. A long crack in smooth granite would not be appropriate, since it would be too constraining. Best is a fairly broad face, generally of lower angle and with plenty of holds, featured with a steeper step here, a smoother slab there, and the occasional ledge and overhang. There must be plenty of choices as to where to go, what feature to ascend. One must be free to choose a more difficult way than the easiest, if that is what strikes the fancy of the moment. The rock must be a menu, for this "menu-soloing." The choices, freedom, movement, mental acuity inspired by the exposure, warmth of the sun, feel of the rock -- the EXPERIENCE is everything.

For me to practice menu-soloing properly, I needed milder selections than what this rock was immediately presenting. Looking across to the exposed corner, I decided I'd be ascending the easiest way I could find and would console myself by clinging with approximately twice the force that was actually needed to keep me attached. Not so for John. He climbed lightly and quickly, with complete confidence. He was always way up ahead of me, either happily entertaining himself with his selections or patiently waiting for me as I slowly and carefully made my way to his position. I think he could have climbed this thing four times in the time it took me.

John pointed out some of the items he had found satisfying in the past. He showed me a slab that one time had exactly fit his appetite, which he thought was perhaps 5.9. It was just to my left, ten feet out from the relatively comfortable dihedral I was in, with 500 feet of exposure. Since it appeared to have no holds, it certainly looked at least 5.9. If I went there, I knew I'd be biting off more than I could chew.

To know John is to know that he climbed that slab precisely because it WAS what suited his appetite at the time. Whether I or anyone else ever knew that he had climbed it was entirely an aside. Social goals, the desire for this or that accomplishment, this or that gain in the hierarchy among one's peers--all of that, I think, has receded for John as he has focused intensely on pure internal experience.

John penned an essay in 1979, "Bouldering: A Mystical Art Form," in which he wrote of "internal" aspects of bouldering and rock climbing in contrast to social, or "outer," aspects. One thing particularly impressive about John's bouldering is that he took difficulty so far, when in his case it has been generated so largely by internal motivation. I wouldn't say his motivation has always been ENTIRELY internal--he is human after all--but the level of difficulty that a boulderer is able to enjoy without regard to social reward seems one good measure of ability.

Chris Jones on the Mental Block, Fort Collins, photo by Rich Littlestone

In the fall of 1987, my wife, Alicia, and I were watching John as he balanced delicately in a tenuous position on a nearly holdless, gently overhanging face in the hills west of Pueblo. His toes were edging on tiny flakes, and his fingers were pulling on equally tiny flakes. After gathering a certain stability, his right arm shot to a high hold. On this route, which John had climbed some years earlier and had repeated several times, there is an almost irresistible tendency for the left hand and both feet to lose their place once the high hold is caught. Still strong enough, at age 50, to hold onto the high hold with his right arm in a one-arm pull, John held on after his feet and left hand came away from their micro-flakes.

Then he quickly dropped back to the ground. "Well, I've pulled my bicep." He said it so matter-of-factly that I figured what he meant was that he tore some muscle tissue--which sounded bad enough. But in fact the tendon attachment at his elbow had pulled entirely away, and he knew it immediately. It was a very painful injury, surely the kind to end a bouldering career at his age, yet he did not complain. He simply held the arm immobile, even maintained a relatively cheerful disposition, as we drove to the emergency room.

Hopefully John won't mind too much if I bring a device from the "outer" world of climbing--difficulty ratings--into what I want to say now. The route on which he injured himself has only been climbed by one other boulderer (Curt Shannon). I was not able to climb it myself. I think it must be about V7--in the modern bouldering rating system--and an unusually technical one.

In his last years of severe dynamic bouldering, John worked on another route in the same granite area--a route that is certainly at least V9. His best attempt was better than what anyone else has been able to do on the route. I have no doubt that John would eventually have climbed this V9 had he not been injured. And I suspect that it would have been all the same to him whether or not anyone ever knew he was still able to climb something so difficult. No one else I know would work on a route this difficult without being driven, at least in part, by a powerful social current.

On the Fatted Calf boulder, west of Pueblo, there is an overhanging groove, on which John was able to pull laterally, do a technical dynamic spring to a hold over the lip, hang on with one hand, and pull over the top (mid-1970's). This route is also about V9. Jim Holloway is the only other boulderer who has climbed it.

John didn't mind telling me that this was a route that he did spend a number of days learning before the ascent. When I asked him how many days this was, his reply was "maybe 5 or 6." Of course, 5 or 6 days is far fewer than used on the most difficult routes (Jim Holloway spent as many as thirty days working his masterpiece V11's). Without any real competition in the 1960's, and plenty of virgin bouldering to be done, it was very rare for John to spend more than one to three days working a route. This is the reason that John did not create a great many V8's and V9's, and tended to work in the V5 to V7 range primarily. Few boulderers or sport climbers today, with training methods and rock gyms, can match how quickly John, with his dedication to training, was able to climb most of his routes. For example, John climbed all three of the main routes on the Mental Block west of Fort Collins--the Left, Center, and Right (Pinch Overhang)--in a single day in late 1968.

Gill on what he calls his most difficult route in Pueblo
(static attempt)

Gill's most difficult route in Pueblo (dynamic ascent)

Then there were the "routines" (as opposed to "routes") that John did, where he would make use of his shoulder-arm-finger power--a power that still is not possessed by any of today's top boulderers and sport climbers. For example, just to the left of the V9 route on the Fatted Calf is a route on which, after reaching a high, sloping, fingertip hold with his right hand, his left hand still down low, John would make a point to not put his feet back on the rock. From this hang he would do a slow one-arm pullup on the sloping fingertip hold until his left hand was over the lip, on which he could do another one-arm pullup before manteling. Even today, in this age of sport climbing, there are no standards by which to apply a rating to such a routine.

With the strength to do up to three full one-arm pullups on a five-eighths-inch, flat surface with his wrist forward, it is amazing that John also acquired the fine technique that allowed him to climb all the delicate, technical problems that he has. In the years since boulderers and rock climbers first became aware of the strength to which John trained himself, there have been just a few who have trained their strength to something near his. Each can attest that it is very difficult to acquire the best footwork when strength alone allows one to solve so many problems. Yet there was John: delicately poised on those tiny flakes just prior to the move which pulled his bicep.

A year after the surgery to re-attach his tendon, John was able to do a one-arm pullup with either arm once again. Not wishing to risk another serious injury from dynamic bouldering, however, he has focused on his particularly internal form of soloing. I see him now, on the rock far above me, a solitary figure, a free and inventive mind engaged in pure experience.

In an essay published in *The Climbing Art* magazine in the fall of '91, Gill encouraged other middle-aged climbers to try option-soloing. The essay's first paragraph:

"Each year the approach of summer rejuvenates me. Academic activities and their attendant social vexations are swept by a cleansing mental tide, and I contemplate the rhapsodic days of solitary climbing that lie ahead. In the best spirit of play I remove myself from undertakings that have purpose, and focus on one that has only meaning."

It has meant a great deal to Gill to be able to look out into the vast expanse of prairie around his home, to see blue sky, or distant peaks with snow, and see the horizon in any direction. He has come to appreciate the prairie itself, hawks, coyotes, the fragrance of sage and brown earth.... A given evening, moonlight brightens the prairie and the sky almost to daylight, and one can see infinitely.

While director of personnel working full time at Parkview Episcopal Hospital, Dorothy finished her bachelor's degree in business by attending Regis College in Colorado Springs. Gill observed to me, about Dorothy:

"She has an amazing amount of energy, commitment, and perseverance. She's thinking now of getting a master's degree. I'm extremely proud of the way things have developed for her, what she's done with her professional life. Alongside her busy career, she has managed to raise her children and my child--for Pam was staying with us full time during one period. Dorothy was never a climber--she knew nothing about climbing when I met her. I took Dorothy, her children, and Pam out to a local area and showed them what rock climbing was all about, put them on a rope, and we had a reasonably good time, but Dorothy had no interest in rock climbing. I have never put pressure on anyone to learn to climb."

John and Dorthy, standing near their prarie home in Pueblo West

John spoke of Dorothy's accomplishments, how Parkview Hospital is a leader in translating Dr. Edward Deming's philosophy to health care and how Dorothy has been to meetings with quality gurus at GM and Ford and spoken with Dr. Deming.

She was born in Budapest in August of 1938, her father a prominent architect, designer, and member of parliament. Dorothy, her two older sisters, and her mother and father were evacuated just before the end of World War II and resettled in the small Bavarian village of Neureichenau, near the Czechoslovakian and Austrian borders. While there, she lived a Heidi-like life--complete with wooden shoes--for five years. In 1950, her family found a sponsor in Billings, Montana, and Dorothy lived there until she left for college. Dorothy's father, Eugene Padanyi-Gulyas, a fascinating, highly intelligent gentleman, lived under a Soviet death threat for many years as a result of participating in Admiral Horthy's Government. Eugene showed an avid interest in mathematics, and both he and John were fond of the writings of Tielhard de Chardin. Gill had several long conversations with Eugene on philosophical matters before Eugene died in 1980. John's own father died in 1978.

John and Dorothy journeyed to Neureichenau in August of 1990 and spent several days in a lodge overlooking a community swimming lake. They hiked and visited places Dorothy remembered, including the large farmhouse where she and her family occupied one room, a very sentimental time for Dorothy. They then drove to Hungary and explored the country while John participated in an international conference on approximation theory at Kecskemet.

John, a full professor since 1981, was awarded the 1991 Provost's Award for Excellence in Scholarship by the University of Southern Colorado. He has published a number of mathematical research papers and is the founder and managing editor of the *International Journal: Communications In The Analytic Theory Of Continued Fractions*. He also served on the National Board of Governors of the Mathematical Association of America.

Dorothy wasted no time in becoming a vice president at Parkview Episcopal Hospital--quite a progression from entry-level bookkeeper.

Pam Gill with John's mother, Bernice

Pam Gill, living in New York City, found a profession in real estate management.

Dorothy's daughter, Susan, made Pueblo her home, in the prairie not far from John and Dorothy, with her son, Dylan. Dorothy's son, Chris, living in the Bay Area, became father to a daughter who, according to Dorothy, "is as petite as Dylan is all boy." John and Dorothy have loved being grandparents to a two-year-old and living close enough to spend time with "this energetic little sprogue" (as John calls Dylan). In return, Dylan has conferred upon the distinguished John Gill the name of "Gumby."

Dylan, John, and Collette, Pueblo, late 1991

Gill's friend Curt Shannon likens grandpa Gumby to "a normal guy:

> He could be the guy standing next to you in line at the supermarket. Your odds of this are greatly enhanced if you buy your groceries in Pueblo. Although he is one of the few genuine legends in the world of climbing, establishing the bench marks by which generations of boulderers will be measured, a remarkable thing about John Gill is how unremarkable he at first appears. When at home, and not working on his new mathematical journal, he can often be found reading, playing catch with the dog, or participating in likewise non-legendary stuff. At his home one evening prior to a post-bouldering-session dinner, for example, his grandson, Dylan, was racing around the concrete with a fire truck--obviously en route to at least a five alarm blaze. Gill was in hot pursuit of Dylan in order to save the catfish which in this instant were certainly an endangered species, balanced as they were on top of the grill. Every time I see Dylan over at John's house, I try not to think about being out-bouldered by somebody's grandfather.
>
> Most people have had the opportunity to watch Olympic caliber gymnastics, if not in person then at least via broadcast into their living room. At this level of the sport, the gymnast is required to perform maneuvers which approach the limits of what is humanly possible while at the same time making them look effortless and almost trivial. "Why, I bet I could do that," sometimes occurs to a misled viewer if the gymnast has been particularly flawless in his execution. On my first visit to Little Owl Canyon with Gill, substitute Gill for the gymnast (me for the viewer). You should, by now, have a fairly good idea what happened. I came away disappointed yet inspired, having succeeded at very little, in spite of the fact that nothing Gill showed me that day looked very hard.
>
> That experience had a tremendous impact on my development as a boulderer, as have all of my subsequent outings with Gill. After finally making it across the Ripper Traverse, in a style that did a great disservice to one of his masterpieces, I remember Gill commenting that my technique was "effective." He can always put a positive twist on my sometimes less than stellar efforts.

Curt Shannon on the Ripper Traverse, Pueblo

I was attempting the second ascent of the problem that ended Gill's dynamic bouldering, and John was there taking photos. The "Micro-Shield" problem, as it's called, involves a very difficult dynamic move from an iron-cross position on razor blade holds to what is essentially the summit. All kinds of thoughts were going through my head. How bad do I want this problem? This move detached Gill's bicep. Not that my bicep is anything to brag about, but I am figuratively and still quite literally attached to it and want it to stay that way.

I went for it. After completing the route and scrambling down the rock's backside, John commented, "Well somebody had to do it, and it may as well have been you."

In 1991, *Climbing Magazine* reported that John Sherman had made the second solo ascent of Gill's Thimble route in the Needles. Sherman was somewhat embarrassed by this account, for he did not claim to have made the second ascent. This was the magazine's claim. The history of the Thimble subsequent to Gill's remarkable ascent was, in fact, uncertain, borne of stories that the route had been done by Pete DeLannoy, and by an eastern climber, or by "some southern kid," possibly by Eric Zschiesche (sp?) from North Carolina, after top-roping, and possibly by Chris Klein (also, it was said, from North Carolina), or by Keith Pike, or by Brent Kertzman....

Pete DeLannoy did in fact solo the route in August of 1987. Seven years earlier, he had tried the route on top-rope as a beginner in the company of Kevin Bein but failing at it. During those seven years, he trained and bouldered a lot. One day in the Needles, not thinking he would solo the route, he saw it and felt the inspiration to try it. He succeeded. So much time had passed between this ascent and his top-rope attempt as a neophyte, that it could hardly be classified as a "rehearsed ascent." DeLannoy remembers getting to the top and feeling proud but wishing that the ascent had not been tainted by his previous top-rope attempt of the route--even if long ago.

A day after this ascent, DeLannoy was astonished to watch "a climber from North Carolina" climb it solo twice. The climber received no advice from DeLannoy and apparently had not tried the route before. This person was, according to DeLannoy, "a character who had long arms and had a cat on a leash." DeLannoy recalls how, on that climber's second time up the route, the person was shaking so bad that it seemed he was going to hit the pavement. When told of this ascent, Gill said with a chuckle, "I'm glad someone did it who was from the South."

A rumor that a 1984 solo of the route had been made by Brent Kertzman was something at least a couple of local Needles climbers doubted, since "such an ascent did not seem in keeping with Brent's ability at the time."

Steve Mammen, Scott Blunk, Kevin Bein, Paul Muehl, Chris Jones, Rich Littlestone, and most likely a good number of other climbers have over the years done a close version of the route with a top-rope and agreed that the climbing is difficult whatever the exact combination of holds used and even with the immense psychological help of a belay from above. In the process of these ascents, it is believed by several climbers, a few holds (or pebbles) have broken off. Yet Pete DeLannoy believes that most if not all of the broken holds have occurred on the lower half of the route rather than on the more difficult upper half.

As to Gill's exact line of ascent, several climbers had gone on the word of the late Kevin Bein who some years prior to his death claimed to have spoken with Gill and was told, according to Needles local climber John Page, that the route moved left (into the groove of the left-hand route) after reaching the point where the climber is standing on the "hold of commitment" halfway up the wall. Gill is certain that he did not say this, but he did tell Kevin that he may have used a hold on the right outside corner of the groove as a left handhold. Pete DeLannoy recalls Kevin saying that Gill called anything with the left hand "game." Perhaps this was the origin of John Page's misconception.

After Sherman made an ascent of the line thought to be proper by Page, Sherman phoned Gill and was told by Gill that an effort was made to avoid the left hand groove the whole way. The ridgeline was gained at a point above where the groove topped out. The two routes then merged, according to Gill, for a brief scramble to the summit. After talking to Gill, Sherman told John Page what he had learned. Oddly, as Sherman discovered, Page had difficulty believing that the line stayed out of the groove. But Sherman returned to the route and climbed it as closely to Gill's directions as possible.

John Sherman climbing the Thimble, 1991

Gill stated in a letter to me in February 1992:

"Although I do not recall the exact placement of holds on the upper part, the entire purpose of my climb--a private challenge--was to avoid as much as possible the other easier climb, without putting myself in extreme jeopardy. That I planned a pure line in the middle of the face is erroneous. I felt that was too dangerous. The way I went, I could have moved at one point into the easy groove--an escape exit (shades of option-soloing?). This just tipped the psychological balance enough for me to commit to a distinct set of moves to the shoulder above. I do recall there was some crystal I pinched out on the face with my right hand. Perhaps it's gone now. Who knows?"

Sherman admitted that the deadly guard railing had been removed (and was gone prior to all of the several "repeat" ascents). He had the benefit of knowing that the route could be climbed. He wore climbing shoes vastly superior to those used in 1961 by Gill. And the large number of competitive boulderers of the modern age certainly sharpened the general consciousness and intensity of a given boulderer's efforts. Sherman had, in addition, the slight psychological edge of a 2-foot-by-3-foot, padded carpet-patch he placed at the bottom of the rock.

Sherman's own strict integrity was to question whether he stayed on the final terrifying move or moves at the top. He may himself have joined the left-hand, easier route a hold or two early. He stated in a letter to Gill, "I joined that route at the shoulder where it becomes trivial."

Perhaps it is a small tribute to Gill that a little mystery should remain. In his usual faith-instilling manner, Gill was happy to give Sherman full credit for the ascent. Throughout his climbing, Gill was never uncomfortable with the success of other people. Here again, it pleased him to share with another climber the exhilaration of having done something remarkable.

In February 1992, while walking through the University of Southern Colorado campus, Gill climbed several extremely smooth cement structures--ribs that had challenged him years before when he was in stronger shape. These involved cross-pressure and friction techniques at a true gymnastic level of difficulty. With Dorothy in a mood for taking photographs, John also climbed up to a high horizontal bar and pulled into a perfect front-lever.

Difficult rib on University of Southern Colorado campus

Grandpa Gumby, front lever

The muscles of his body were sore for several days after, but he learned something. The joy of attempting these difficult moves made the forty years that he had been climbing vanish.

148

Rocky Mountain National Park, Colorado, in the '60s

Gill's Crack, Devil's Lake, Wisconsin, mid '60s

Devil's Lake

Dixon Springs, Southern Illinois (three photos, lower photo "Jumbo")

Hagermeister Boulders, near Estes Park, Colorado, early 1960's

Hagermeister Boulders

Hagermeister Boulders

Hagermeister Boulders

Rocky Mountain National Park area, Colorado, in the early '60s (Whiskey Bottle Rock, near Estes)

Near Estes (the Right Side of the Rat's Tooth on Twin Owls and Little Dome)

Near Estes (the Block)

158

Near   Estes   (Angel
Overhang)

Near Estes, along the Gem Lake Trail (four photos)

Split Rocks, Colorado (Gill, Ament), the Delicate Wall, mid-60s

Split Rocks, Colorado

Split Rocks

Split Rocks

Split Rocks

Split Rocks

Split Rocks, a difficult mantel

Tetons, Cufinger Rock (route
done with one-arm)

The Needles of South Dakota

The Needles

The Needles, early '70s, position reached by free aerial move

The Needles

The Needles

The Needles

The Needles

The Needles

Elephant Rocks, Missouri, 1967

Elephant Rocks

Elephant Rocks

City of Rocks, Idaho, mid and late-'60s

Flagstaff Mountain, Boulder, Colorado

Gill's Boulder, in the west end of Eldorado Canyon, Colorado, late '60s

Eldorado Canyon, late '60s (Milton Boulder)

Montana, Beartooth Range, 1976

Southern Wyoming, Snowy Range, near Lake Marie, early '70s

Veedauwoo, Wyoming, late '60s

Veedauwoo, Wyoming

184

Veedauwoo

Veedauwoo

Veedauwoo

Fort Collins, Colorado (near Horse Tooth Reservoir)

Fort Collins

Fort Collins

Fort Collins

Fort Collins

Fort Collins

Fort Collins

John Gill at Fort Collins, in the late '60s

John Gill, Fort Collins, mid '70s

About Pat Ament, by John Gill

When Pat Ament suggested in 1976 that he do a book about my climbing activities, I was delighted. For here was a superbly skilled rock climber with exceptional writing talent who also was an innovative and inspiring boulderer--a combination of attributes unique in my experience. It was clear that it takes a boulderer to understand the unusual and devious nature of the sport. When Pat first coined the phrase "the poetry of mountaineering," it was apparent that he had a deep appreciation for the less obvious. In fact, it takes an actual poet to truly appreciate the more subtle qualities of bouldering. A number of his boulder problems on Flagstaff Mountain above Boulder and in Yosemite Valley remain test pieces and show an ability to articulate his poetic spirit through a stubborn medium.

Though we live in an age of specialization, Pat embodies the essence of Europe's high Renaissance. He is at once a very sensitive poet, a somewhat extensively published essayist, an editor, a teacher of writing, an award-winning filmmaker, an award-winning artist of line drawings, a still-photographer, a chess expert, a noted chess problem-composer published in Grandmaster columns, a pianist and songwriter, an extremely well-regarded mentor for the young (both in climbing and in chess), a long-time member of Shotokan Karate of America, and an internationally-recognized climber who continues to perform at quite high levels today.

Pat has also been my good friend for over twenty years. We met in Fort Collins and bouldered together in halcyon days when our bodies were thinner and our deeds more nearly matched our visions.

Pat is devoted to a spiritual life, although he moves occasionally through minor squalls of controversy. He weathers them well. For me, they symbolize merely the ripples made by an enduring creative personality, a true individual in a sea of conformity.